M000046002

SAVING SANDOVAL

THE TRUE STORY OF AN ARMY SNIPER CHARGED WITH MURDER ON THE BATTLEFIELD

CRAIG W. DRUMMOND

WILDB<small>LUE</small>

P R E S S

WildBluePress.com

SAVING SANDOVAL published by:
WILDBLUE PRESS
P.O. Box 102440
Denver, Colorado 80250

WILDBLUE PRESS is registered at the U.S. Patent and Trademark Offices.

ISBN 978-1-942266-78-5 Trade Paperback

ISBN 978-1-942266-75-4 eBook

Interior Formatting/Book Cover Design by Elijah Toten www.totencreative.com

SAVING SANDOVAL ENDORSEMENTS

"It's a story that I'm sure the government would like us all to forget," said WildBlue Press Owner and *New York Times* Bestselling Author Steve Jackson. *"Craig has done an outstanding job, both as an attorney fighting for a young soldier's freedom, and documenting what happened."*

"Armed forces continue to operate in uncertain and complex environments and this story is an insightful and powerful look into the challenges and judgments faced by a young sniper deployed to the battlefield of Iraq."— Brigadier General Jeffery L. Underhill, U.S. Army Retired, (Iraq Veteran)

"After the Iraq invasion, a military lawyer tests military justice by defending an American soldier accused of a war crime. A revealing, real life, courtroom drama, reminiscent of A Few Good Men."—Professor Hunter R. Clark, Director, International Law and Human Rights Program, Drake University Law School

"This book is a strong caution for all military commanders who would consider judging the warriors who run towards to sound of gunfire. Front-line actions should be judged from a front-line perspective, not for how those actions may play in the news."—Dave Earp, former U.S. Navy SEAL Officer, USNA '97, BUDS Class #230, (Iraq and Afghanistan Veteran)

*"**Saving Sandoval** gives an inside look at the scrutiny Soldiers face on the battlefield and the politics involved in modern day warfare."*—Major Chris Ophardt, U.S. Army, Public Affairs Officer to the Secretary of the Army, 2016-2017, (Iraq Veteran)

This book is dedicated to
my wife, my two boys, and my parents
for always being there and
standing as the guideposts of my life.

ACKNOWLEDGMENTS

I want to extend my immense thanks to Jorge G. Sandoval, Jr. for authorizing me to tell our complete story.

I also want to acknowledge and extend my appreciation to all the men and women who have served and are serving our country in combat operations since the attacks of September 11, 2001. War as we know it in the history books has changed, and the battlefields and rules are no longer clear. To the men and women continuing to answer our nation's call, we owe you more than we have given.

FOREWORD

I sat down to write this book in 2008 as I was beginning to think about leaving the Army. The memories of my time in Iraq and my representation and defense of Specialist Jorge G. Sandoval, Jr., were beginning to fade, and I wanted to capture them and commit them to paper before they were too long gone to recall. So, I began to gather my notes, emails, transcripts, statements, and all the evidence from the case and started writing. Then, well, life got in the way.

The book was shelved in 2010 as I transitioned from being an Army lawyer to the civilian practice of law, eventually starting my own law firm. Marriage, children, clients, and trials all stood in the way of completing this book and telling this story. On New Year's Eve of 2015, my wife asked me what my goal was for the coming year, and I said, "To finish the book," to which she replied, "Then you had better get started!"

Sandoval's story is one that should be told, and as Americans, lawyers, and those interested in military history, we can hopefully learn something from it. This is a story of injustice but it is also a story of being able to rectify part of the injustice and as such it provides hope for our future.

A NOTE ABOUT REFERENCES AND SOURCES

This book is derived from my best recollection as well as review of thousands of pages of notes, emails, transcripts, and statements. Furthermore, this book includes interview material derived from interviews between my personal editor, Vivien Cooper, and Jorge G. Sandoval, Jr., in early 2016. Ms. Cooper provided invaluable assistance helping me to tell this story and the interviews were conducted by Ms. Cooper because we thought it would be important to hear Sandoval's words from his mouth to a stranger rather than he and I simply reminiscing about our time in Iraq and the reader being on the sideline of that conversation.

All quoted material is verbatim to the best of my knowledge. There are some statements and testimony where a minor word was changed to clarify something, or for the sake of brevity, or where it was not clear what the original handwritten word actually was from reading a handwritten statement. Certain sections of statements and transcripts were deleted to be more concise and to delete minute legal objections and other procedural actions and arguments during trial in the case. It would have been impractical to include the entirety of the immense casefile by listing every witness statement, every legal issue and all the transcripts of testimony. It is not believed that any of the changes are substantive in any manner and were made simply to focus on the key points of the quoted testimony and the key facts of the case and Sandoval's story.

This book was not written as a law review article or scholarly publication. As such, detailed footnoting has not been completed for every reference. However, I have retained the complete casefile from my representation of Sandoval should any of the information or quotations in this book ever be challenged.

Finally, there is mention in this book that a portion of the trial itself was closed to the public to address classified evidence. This is true. However, this book does not contain any information I was ever notified was classified or that I received via classified means or with classified markings. The references to classified evidence at the trial are taken from the public transcript and references from that transcript only. Furthermore, early in the defense of the case in 2007, I sent an email to the Trial Counsel, the representative of the United States government in the case, and I have in my file the response I received outlining what information in the case was not classified. It is only such unclassified evidence that is referenced and cited in this book.

I have done my best to ensure that this book presents the whole truth. After all, the truth best tells the real story of Sandoval's case. The citations, references, conclusions, and judgments made in this book are mine, and I am solely responsible for their fairness and accuracy.

TABLE OF CONTENTS

ONE - THE ARREST

"The sniper must be able to calmly and deliberately kill targets that may not pose an immediate threat to him. It is much easier to kill in self-defense or in the defense of others than it is to kill without apparent provocation."

~ *"Sniper Training," U.S. Army Field Manual 23-10 (1994)*

On 26 June 2007, two United States Army Criminal Investigation Command (CID) Agents quietly approached the front door of a home in Laredo, Texas, and knocked. Their mission: to arrest U.S. Army sniper, Specialist Jorge Sandoval, Jr.

Specialist Sandoval recalled in a 2016 interview:

"It was only a few days after my twenty-second birthday when the agents showed up. I was home on leave from Iraq and excited to be home to spend my birthday with my family. I was at my mom's house, doing some push-ups and working out. Mom was in the kitchen making lunch. It surprised me to hear a knock on the door because I hadn't heard any vehicles approaching the house.

I answered the door and was greeted by two gentlemen wearing polo shirts and cargo pants. They identified themselves as Army CID Agents and asked me, "Are you Specialist Jorge Sandoval, Jr.?"

"Yes." I said, "What is this about?" I stepped outside and that's when I saw two vehicles—an unmarked vehicle and a police vehicle with lights flashing.

"We need to ask you some questions related to an incident that occurred while you were in Iraq. We will need you to accompany us to the police station for questioning."

"Fine. Just let me go inside and get dressed," I said.

I quickly changed my clothes, and when my mom saw that I had changed, she asked me where I was going. "*Adonde vas, mijo?*"

I responded in Spanish, saying, "Look, I don't know... some people want to talk to me. I don't know what it's about. When I find out what's going on, I'll let you know... but I must tell you, I don't know if I'm coming back.'

As the agents were escorting me away from the house I thought, *Maybe something happened with one of my friends in Iraq.* I assumed I was getting into their unmarked vehicle with them so I began to move toward the car door to open it.

"No," they said, stopping me. "You're not going to ride in this vehicle."

Two local police officers blocked off both sides of the road, put my hands behind my back, put me in handcuffs, and put me into the back of a squad car.

That was the moment I first started to realize that I was in some type of custody. *Okay, so this definitely has something to do with me,* I thought, *not one of my friends. What could have happened? Why am I being taken into custody? Did I do something wrong?*

As I tried to get a grasp of the situation, all sorts of things were going through my mind. I traveled back in my memory to Iraq, quickly flipping through my recollections of various dates, trying to get a sense of what was happening to me. I thought back to the events that led to me and a few friends of mine finding ourselves in sniper positions in the U.S. Army.

As the squad car pulled away from my mom's house with me inside, I thought, *This is terrible timing! Michelle's waiting for me, and she's going to think I stood her up.* Michelle was a childhood friend and we had just recently reconnected and started dating. I knew I couldn't text her from the squad car.

When we got to the police station, I was put in an interrogation room and my phone was placed on the table in front of me. It immediately started ringing. I knew it was Michelle.

For two hours, an interrogation was conducted by one of the CID Agents who had come to my mother's door and a female agent who had stayed in the unmarked vehicle as I was being picked up. They interrogated me about missions I had undertaken in Iraq during April and May of 2007. The phone continued to ring and ring, but I was forbidden to answer it.

I tried to answer their questions to the fullest of my ability. At no point during the interrogation did they reveal to me why I was being held and questioned. Finally, their questioning started to wind down, so I asked, "Am I free to go? Can I leave now? And, can I please have my phone back?"

The two agents glanced at each other and then one of them said, "No, son. You're going back to the theater." [1]

"Back to the theater?" Back to *Iraq?* I couldn't believe they were sending me back to the Middle East.

"Okaaaayyy..." I said, still in the dark as to what was going on.

One of them handed me back my phone. "I am giving you one call. I recommend you call your parents. Have them pack a bag for you and meet you here."

I had been handcuffed, taken to the police station in a squad car, interrogated, and had my phone taken away. Now I was being sent back to the theater. By this point, I had put two and two together. *They're not sending me back to fight. I'm going to be spending time in prison somewhere.*

---

1   Theater is the term used to describe a "theater of war" or "theater of operations" and can encompass an entire area of armed conflict including actual battlefields and surrounding area; for example, Iraq.

"Listen," I told my mother in Spanish when I got her on the phone, "you need to pack a bag for me. Can you grab my assault backpack—the pack that looks like it's from the Army? Put everything that looks like it's from the Army in there and bring it to me at the police station."

When I was taken out to the main entrance of the police station to wait for my mom to arrive with my pack, I was surprised to see my entire family waiting there to say goodbye to me. They all had very serious expressions on their faces.

My mother must have hung up with me and then quickly called my father. (They had been separated since I was four years old.) She must have also called my two sisters. I hated for them to see me in that situation, but I was grateful for the chance to say goodbye.

"Say your goodbyes quickly," the agents told me. They gave me the feeling that I was going away and not coming back.

My family asked me in Spanish what was going on. I told them, "These people are from the military. There's something going on..."

Before saying goodbye to my family, I had been shown the charge sheet from my Army commander so I knew exactly what was going on. The charge sheet stated:

Charge I: Violation of the UCMJ, Article 118... The Specification: *In that Specialist Jorge G. Sandoval, Jr., did, at or near Abu Shemsi, Iraq, on or about 27 April, 2007, murder an Iraqi national by means of shooting him with a rifle.*

Charge II: Violation of the UCMJ, Article 134... The Specification: *In that Specialist Jorge G. Sandoval, Jr., did, at or near Jurf as Sakhr, Iraq, on or about*

11 May, 2007, wrongfully place command wire2 with the remains of Genei Nesir Khudair Al-Janabi, which conduct was to the prejudice of good order and discipline in the armed forces or of a nature to bring discredit upon the armed forces.

♦ ♦ ♦

I recalled doing my final preparations for the 27 April 2007 mission. Although I had been on missions before, it was going to be my first or second mission as a sniper, and I had the nervous feeling everyone gets in advance of a mission. As we moved closer to the start time of that mission, I felt the nerves and jitters and tried to consider all the possibilities and anticipate what could happen. From the time you actually leave the gate of the base, you put all that aside and focus on your mission and your objectives.

I believe that Sergeant Hensley and I took off around one in the morning, and then the rest of the team took off twenty or thirty minutes behind us. Since I had gone on the initial recon of the area, Sergeant Hensley made me the point person of our team. I felt confident with GPS and knew where we were going and what we were doing.

Sergeant Hensley and I understood each other. We knew what to do. From the time we received the warning order[3], we already knew what to ask and what to do when it came to packing. Based on how many days we'd be gone, we knew

---

2   Command wire is normal electrical wire but is commonly used by insurgents in rigging improvised explosive devices (IEDs) and other types of bombs to attack U.S. and coalition forces.

3   A warning order, or WARNO, is the term for an order issued by the military command concerning an upcoming mission. A warning order is normally general in nature and issued as soon as possible to give the date, time, and known information about the mission so that preparations can begin. A warning order is normally followed by a formal operations order providing specific details concerning the mission.

how much water we would need because we had learned from other missions where we ran out of water or food. We were past that stage where we needed other people to look after us.

Our mission was to interdict the mortar team attacking friendly units in our area of responsibility. I felt confident up until we made it to a certain point where we hadn't yet done recon in the area. So, we got to this one area and I remember there being this good-sized canal filled with water. We couldn't seem to find a way across it but we had to continue our mission and get to our objective regardless.

Sergeant Hensley found what looked like a good spot to cross and said, "Oh, hey, we could cross it right through here." "Okay, I said, "Sounds good."

In the dark of the early morning, Sergeant Hensley went into the canal before me, carrying his assault pack with his sustainment for the seventy-two-hour mission. I was carrying a rucksack with a ton of water along with our mission equipment radios and a bunch of other stuff. You waterproof everything as much as you can, but there's only so much you can do.

I pulled security as Sergeant Hensley crossed.

"Oh, man, this canal is so deep!" he said.

He is six-foot-three or four, so the water only came up to his upper chest and neck area. Watching him and knowing I'm only five-foot-eight, I thought, *Crossing this is going to suck for me!*

Sure enough, I was completely submerged from head to toe. The only thing I was able to keep above my head was my rifle. Everything else went into the canal with me. When I finally reached the other side of the canal, I threw my rifle up on the bank and came up with my hand sticking out. I assumed Sergeant Hensley would give me a hand, but he was so focused on the mission that once he saw that I was almost out of the canal, he turned and started walking.

At the time I thought, *What the hell?!* But I knew why he kept going. He was just focused on the mission. The two of us understood each other. Not just the two of us—the sniper section in general.

I managed to grab hold of some tall vegetation on the bank and pull myself out, but I lost so much energy, it took a while to regain my bearings. As soon as I was out of the canal, I saw a house and heard some dogs barking. *This is not good,* I said to myself.

I looked through my night vision goggles and there was Sergeant Hensley about fifty meters away, still walking. Since he hadn't waited for me or stuck around to make sure I'd made it out of the canal without drowning, I had no other choice but to catch up.

We reached the rendezvous rally point where we were supposed to meet the other team that had set out twenty minutes after us. Once they showed up, I noticed they were totally dry, head to toe. They had found a crossing further up the canal and crossed there. I couldn't believe it.

We all sat together for three to five minutes, made a map check, and sent up our present position to let higher command know we were moving on to our objective overwatch. All the while, I was still trying to get my breath back from the canal crossing. I had damn near drowned and was exhausted. Then about another 200 meters into our movement, I rolled my ankle. It was only the first night of a seventy-two-hour mission and already I'd nearly drowned and rolled my ankle. My ankle had been bad from the start as I broke it in high school, and it never fully healed.

What kept going through my head was the fact that I'd heard dogs barking when I got out of the canal. All I could think was, *Hopefully we won't get attacked!*

Sergeant Hensley and I separated from the others.

I believe two other sniper teams with .50 caliber sniper rifles went off to their own hide-site[4] and me and Hensley continued on our way to ours. Every step I took a step on my badly swollen ankle was agonizing. Once at the hide-site, I threw myself on my rucksack and leaned back on it. I left my boot on as I knew that if I took it off, my ankle would be in worse shape.

It was all business from there. Security was us, just him and me. We set up a sleep plan where we would sleep in one-hour shifts, one hour up and one hour down.

We stood up, surveyed the area, looked around, and then went into our sleep plan. We had already set up all our communications. We were lying down on our stomachs doing our mission and I thought, *As long as we don't do anything and I don't have to move my ankle too much, the swelling will go down.*

We had gotten to our objective around three o'clock that morning, and sunrise would come around six. We were still in our rest plan. We had gotten off to a rough start, but now Sergeant Hensley and I were talking and hanging out, passing the time.

Right around sunrise, we were in our hide-site—a small dry canal—sitting up under a bushy tree. We both heard voices in the area and looked at each other and knew that we were thinking the same thing: "Oh, shit! Somebody's coming!"

We didn't want to pop up and get compromised only hours into our mission. We saw three individuals pass right by the canal. They just walked right by. We didn't think they saw us, so we left it at that. They were males, not that old, maybe in their twenties.

---

4   The location where sniper teams, or other light infantry units, consolidate to rest, pull security and/or fire at the enemy is termed a hide-site, as it is the location where they are hiding.

I knew that whatever happened, I could trust Sergeant Hensley. We totally understood each other. And we knew what to do.

◆ ◆ ◆

As I was saying goodbye to my family, I told them, "I want you to hear this from me before you hear it from anyone else. I am being charged with the murder of an Iraqi man. I just want you to know that I was just doing my job. That's it. Everything's going to be fine."

I kissed my mom on the cheek. "*Te quiero mucho, Mamma. Nos vemos pronto.*"[5]

When I told my family that everything was going to be fine, I didn't necessarily believe it myself. I just wanted to comfort them.

As the CID Agents transported me, I wanted to object and say, "What do you mean you're sending me back to the theater? I've only used up ten of my fifteen days of leave time!"

I knew there was no point. They weren't treating me disrespectfully, but they were definitely treating me as if I had already been convicted of murder.

---

5   "I love you so much Mamma, see you soon."

TWO - A TRIAL
DEFENSE ATTORNEY

"Defending those who defend America."

~ The motto of the U.S. Army Trial Defense
Service (TDS), an independent unit of
defense attorneys in the U.S. Army Judge
Advocate General's Corps (JAG)

I was to serve as the defense attorney for Specialist Jorge Sandoval, Jr. (hereafter referred to simply as Sandoval), who was charged with murdering an Iraqi by shooting him in the head with his .50 caliber sniper rifle. On 22 July 2007, on a pitch-black night not quite a month after CID Agents arrested Sandoval at his mother's house, I found myself being flown by Blackhawk helicopter into the "Triangle of Death." The area had earned its nickname due to the high numbers of attacks on U.S. troops and secular violence in the area since the start of the U.S. occupation of Iraq in 2003. During the 2007 timeframe, the area was living up to its nickname as the U.S. forces in the area were taking heavy losses by the enemy.

I was being flown from the large U.S. airbase of Anaconda, Iraq, to Forward Operating Base Iskandariyah. "FOB Iskan," as it was informally known, was a very small, remote, battalion-level U.S. outpost located near the ancient city of Iskandariyah, twenty-five miles south of Baghdad near the largest power plant in Iraq.

I was headed to FOB Iskan as Sandoval's lead attorney to attend an Article 32 pretrial investigation—a proceeding under the United States Uniform Code of Military Justice (UCMJ), similar to that of a preliminary hearing in civilian law. [6] In the military, serious charges must be investigated by an impartial military officer in an Article 32 hearing before a defendant's case can be referred to a general court-martial.

The UCMJ specifies several different levels of formality by which infractions by U.S. military members can be dealt. The most serious is a general court-martial. A general court-martial is a federal felony-level court where evidentiary rules apply, a military judge presides over the trial, and the accused has the right to a panel to determine innocence or guilt. A military panel is a near equivalent to a civilian jury panel and is comprised of senior officers and soldiers. The foreman, or panel president, is the highest-ranking officer on a military panel. In practice, the terms "military panel" and "jury" are used interchangeably.

At the conclusion of a general court-martial, the accused is sentenced and faces the full range of punishments under the law—in some cases, death. If the accused had chosen to be tried by a military panel, as opposed to just a judge, then the panel also decides the appropriate punishment.

For the Article 32, the Investigating Officer is not usually a JAG Corps officer (military attorneys are known as Judge Advocates or JAGs) but rather a non-attorney officer assigned to review the case from an outsider's perspective. A mid-level officer, typically a Major, is appointed by the Brigade Commander to conduct the investigation. This officer investigates the case, listens to evidence, and makes recommendations to senior military commanders as to what to do.

The purpose of the Article 32 is for the Investigating Officer to make a "thorough and impartial investigation" of the evidence and to "include inquiry as to the truth of the matter set forth in the charges, consideration of the form

---

6   Article 32 is derived from UCMJ Section VII ("Trial Procedure") (10 U.S.C.§832), which mandates the pretrial hearing that must occur before a general court-martial can be held.

of the charges, and a recommendation as to the disposition which should be made of the case in the interest of justice and discipline."

A hearing date is set and the prosecution calls witnesses who testify about any relevant facts that they may know about the case. The regular rules governing the admission of evidence—which would normally control the types of questions that may be asked and what kind of documentary or physical evidence may be introduced in a trial—do not apply. As a result, the Article 32 is considered only a quasi-judicial proceeding.

During the hearing, the Investigating Officer reviews all the evidence, listens to the direct- and cross-examination of witnesses, and then questions the witnesses himself if he desires.

Sandoval was being flown separately under guard from Camp Arifjan in Kuwait to FOB Iskan in Iraq for the Article 32 hearing. The CID Agents who removed Sandoval from his mother's home in Laredo had transported him to Camp Arifjan. Once there, his command had ordered him into pretrial confinement pending trial. By the time I was detailed[7] the case, Sandoval was already in confinement at Camp Arifjan.

"I was surprised," he recalls, "that I did not end up imprisoned in Iraq. Up until then, I hadn't even realized there was a military prison Kuwait."

◆ ◆ ◆

I had started my journey to become an officer and attorney

---

7   Being "detailed" to a case is simply being assigned to defend a specific soldier who has been charged with a crime. Once detailed, the military defense counsel's mission is to defend that soldier. Trial Counsel are also detailed to cases and their role is prosecuting a specific case on behalf of the United States. Normally, once an attorney is detailed a case they remain assigned to the case until completion.

in 1997 as an Army ROTC Cadet at Drake University. When I accepted a full scholarship from the Army, my service consisted of participating in ROTC as a Cadet and then serving four years on active duty and subsequently four years in the Reserves.

Upon receiving my undergraduate degree, I was commissioned as a Second Lieutenant in the Army Reserves and placed in a reserve status where I was allowed to complete law school before my active duty obligation began. Because they gave me a scholarship when they were not common, I stayed at Drake for law school. After the towers fell on September 11, 2001 I felt a strong desire to put on the uniform and was not content sitting on the sidelines after our country had been attacked. I reached out to some Drake alumni who were senior officers in the Iowa Army National Guard and within a few weeks began serving one weekend a month in the Guard assisting with the mobilization of military units for overseas deployment.

Law school was hard but I had some great experiences and learned to love the law by working part-time at a litigation law firm and enrolling in all of the law school's criminal defense clinics. There I had the opportunity to represent indigent criminals in court, practicing law with a student practice license.

After graduation, I moved home to Saint Joseph, Missouri, and for the first time in almost eight years, lived with my parents while I studied for the Missouri Bar exam. After passing the Bar and acceptance into the JAG Corps, I reported for duty at the Army JAG Basic Course in Charlottesville, Virginia. All new Judge Advocates report to the Judge Advocate Generals Legal Center and School (TJAGLCS) for four months to learn military-specific legal topics.

JAG School, as it is informally called, is located in Charlottesville on the grounds of the University of Virginia and is the main training center for Army military and civilian attorneys. The initial training is called the Basic Course; it teaches all sorts of subjects from military justice, family law, estate planning, and regulatory law to the law of war and military operations. Judge Advocates often return to the school each year for continuing legal education courses. It was at JAG School that I first learned the intricacies of the Uniform Code of Military Justice (UCMJ) and the law of war.

After completion of the Basic Course, I headed for Fort Bliss, Texas, and was soon promoted to the rank of Captain. In my role as a Judge Advocate at Fort Bliss, I first worked as a Legal Assistance Attorney helping soldiers and their families with their personal civilian legal problems. Legal Assistance is the Army's equivalent of a legal aid office wherein the attorney does not represent the Army but instead represents the client, working on his or her behalf and assisting on a wide range of issues from simple estate planning and wills to complex consumer law issues.

New attorneys are often assigned as Legal Assistance attorneys for about a year and consider it "purgatory" because the job can feel like temporary punishment. This is since many of the issues presented by legal assistance clients arise due to poor decisions on the part of the soldier or his/her family. One can easily become apathetic, and this is exacerbated by the fact that appointments are scheduled every thirty minutes from 9 a.m. to 5 p.m.

By the end of the day, I would have had about enough of listening to people complain about how awful or unfair the world—or life—is while rarely acknowledging their role in their predicament. It was difficult to remain motivated while attempting to assist those who had dug their own holes into debt or multiple marriages. When dealing with those clients who were truly wronged by someone else, however, it was rewarding to find a solution or right the wrong.

Despite the challenges of working in Legal Assistance, I found it to be a great learning experience. Law school offered classes on client interaction, but working in Legal Assistance was a total immersion course. It was a real-world situation five days a week where a new client was coming in every half hour. I had to learn how to think on my feet, how to instantly relate to strangers, and how to discern what outcome clients really wanted. Then I had to find some sort of answer or guidance for them before they walked out of my office at the end of thirty minutes.

Another thing that made working in Legal Assistance a good experience was the fact that I worked for a great civilian attorney boss who taught me by example. Despite the hectic pace of dealing with so many clients and issues in one day, my boss always seemed to keep a level head. He never got riled up as clients complained to him about their problems or about how the attorney to whom they'd been assigned was unable to perform miracles during their consultation or solve all of their problems. In almost every instance, my boss backed up the attorney.

It was comforting to know that the boss always had your back, if you proceeded as ethically as possible, gave advice that was within your competence level, and declined to give any advice when you were unfamiliar with the issue or could not research it. Of course, in a perfect world, this is the way every law office would be run, but it doesn't always unfold that way. I was friends with plenty of attorneys who would tell horror stories of working in large law firms where they had to tiptoe around every issue out of fear that the boss would disapprove or throw them under the bus if they made even the smallest mistake.

I was fortunate to have had the pleasure of working in an environment where I could advocate for my clients on many levels and through many mediums and be supported in what I was doing. It was a good learning experience in dealing with cases and clients. Nevertheless, after a year of working in Legal Assistance, I was ready to move on.

I transitioned to the role of representing the Army and the United States, prosecuting soldiers for criminal actions. In the position of military prosecutor in the Army, you are called a Trial Counsel and are normally in a position where you advise a Brigade Commander, a Colonel, with all criminal justice cases for his unit. The Trial Counsel typically has two enlisted soldier–paralegals and is responsible for prosecuting cases in court, overseeing criminal investigations, preparing letters of reprimand, and generally supervising the disposition of all misconduct.

In the military, a commander has multiple options when disposing of misconduct. A commander can take no action, can orally reprimand the soldier, reprimand the soldier in writing, initiate non-judicial punishment (known as an Article 15 where some of their pay is taken away for a short period of time or a soldier is lowered in rank), or prefer criminal charges and recommend the case undergo a formal investigation and then potentially a court-martial.

Preferral is the term for charging a service member with a crime wherein one service member—the accuser—fills out a charge sheet, which is basically just a form listing certain information about an alleged criminal act. Once the charge sheet is prepared, the accuser swears to an oath before a military officer that he/she "has personal knowledge, or has investigated the matters set forth therein, and that the same are true to the best of his/her knowledge and belief."

Once the accuser signs the charge sheet and takes the oath, the service member is then considered formally charged with a crime. It is up to the soldier's commander as to how to dispose of the charge and charge sheet.

Charges and charging decisions are normally made in consultation with a commander and the prosecutor, and it is typically the Company Commander who charges his own soldiers with crimes. If someone else charged a commander's soldier with a crime without the commander's knowledge, then, upon learning of the charges, he or she could just dismiss them on the spot and that would be the end of it.

In any given Army unit, only about five percent of all misconduct is generally sent to court-martial. So, while the title of Trial Counsel may imply all sorts of trial experience, the reality is that on many military bases, the job is typically more about overseeing investigations and preparing documents than trying cases. During my time as a Trial Counsel I was fortunate—or unfortunate, depending whether or not you like to stay busy at work—to have a plethora of cases sent to court-martial.

I understood that I was being detailed the Sandoval case based at least partially on my previous experience at Fort Bliss where I had tried a number of contested courts-martial as a Trial Counsel and had also prosecuted a murder case. Thankfully, the Army does not have that many murder prosecutions and so the Judge Advocates who have either prosecuted or defended one are few and far between.

My experience as a Trial Counsel representing the United States had been a true trial by fire. Fort Bliss had been selected to expand and add troops and units based on its massive land size and supportive El Paso community. This also meant that it was regarded as one of the busiest courts-martial jurisdictions in the Army, and the quantity and range of ongoing investigations and trials was in many respects overwhelming for the growing installation. The murder I prosecuted at Fort Bliss was both gruesome and complex. The bottom line is that the soldier had some serious mental health issues which the Army did not know about when he enlisted, and one morning while his wife went shopping, he picked up his four-month-old daughter and threw her against a wall, cracking her skull on both the right and left side and ultimately killing her.

The cause of death was blunt force head trauma. The medical examiner testified at trial that even a fall from a roof would not have enough force to cause the kind of trauma that he inflicted on his daughter's head. The jury found him guilty of involuntary manslaughter and sentenced him to the maximum of ten years' confinement. I felt that the sentence was too lenient and unjust. I suppose at the end of the day, the jury thought that because of his psychiatric issues, he was not fully aware of what he was doing and did not have the criminal intent to kill his daughter. The lesson I learned was that you never know what a jury will do even if you put forth what you think are straightforward facts.

In any contested trial, a good attorney will recognize at least a few things that they could have done differently—introduced this piece of evidence instead of that one, or made a different argument. The important point for me has been to focus on what I did right, or wrong, during any given trial and ensure that in the future I do not repeat the same mistakes.

After thirteen months of prosecuting countless crimes and with five felony jury trials under my belt as a lead prosecutor, I was reassigned from prosecuting soldiers to defending them and was offered the opportunity to deploy to a combat zone to defend soldiers. As most other active-duty soldiers had already deployed to a combat zone in the post–9/11 environment, I jumped at the chance when offered, and the paperwork was started. Although I considered it a great privilege to serve stateside, our country was at war, and I was in uniform and wanted to go to war. That's what I signed up for.

Soon thereafter, I received orders assigning me to the U.S. Army Trial Defense Service (TDS) with immediate orders to deploy to Iraq. TDS is an independent unit within the U.S. Army Judge Advocate General's Corps and is part of the U.S. Army Legal Services Agency (USALSA). The TDS motto: "Defending those who defend America."

On 16 June 2007, I reported to Fort Benning, Georgia for my seven day pre-deployment training. During those seven-days, I was to receive refresher training in combat, marksmanship, and first aid. I was also issued all the military equipment and uniforms that I would need in a combat zone.

Some service members go to Iraq because their entire unit was ordered there, some go as replacements to fill losses for those units already there, and others go as individuals to fill individual slots. I went to Iraq as an individual and was sent to Fort Benning's CONUS (Contiguous United States) Replacement Center (CRC), along with all replacements and individuals deploying. The CRC provides training to soldiers and government contractors going to many countries and locations including Iraq, Afghanistan, Cuba, Kuwait, and others, and has over one hundred service members go through their classes and training every week in preparation for deployment.

During my time at Fort Benning, I underwent medical screenings, vaccines for every possible disease, weapons qualification, uniform issuance, and familiarization with the environment of Iraq. In the middle of the night, I boarded a chartered plane headed to Iraq en route to Balad where the massive joint Air Force and Army base, Logistical Support Area Anaconda (LSA) was located.

Once I arrived in the Middle East, whenever I needed to fly around the region from base to base, I would usually be flying on a standby basis on military aircraft and often found myself sleeping on tent floors and waiting for any flight that had room for an extra passenger. Sometimes that entailed rides on fixed aircraft but just as often I would find myself on helicopters or the most dangerous transportation option of all, ground vehicle convoys on desolate and dangerous highways.

On those flights, I might be flying with civilians, foreign nationals and/or security contractors who were working for the government, and sometimes there were senior members of the Iraqi military. I would be flying into these dangerous areas wearing my Kevlar vest and helmet as well as shatterproof protective eyeglasses. The civilians and private contractors also wore Kevlar bulletproof vests (also called flak vests) over their civilian clothes.

On some of my travels, I was a little bit wary when I would encounter the disheveled-looking civilian who was wearing a helmet that someone had dragged out of a World War II locker and a flak vest that looked like it could be pierced by a bow and arrow. In that region, the enemy wasn't always clear and obvious. I would think to myself, *Obviously, no one cares a great deal about their welfare or considers them to be of particularly high importance to their mission, so who are they exactly? And how well have they been vetted before being allowed to be on this aircraft?*

Balad Air Base, also called Anaconda, is located forty miles north of Baghdad. It was to become my main office, but I would only end up spending a couple of days each week there. I was traveling all over Iraq the rest of the time.

First stop: Ali Al Salem Airfield in Kuwait. That's where all U.S. troops arrived to be processed into Iraq, Afghanistan, or Kuwait and arrange transportation to their duty location. The processing is an important event as it places the soldier on the books as physically being in the country for purposes of command and control.

When the plane from Fort Benning landed in Kuwait, it was 112 degrees F outside and as I deplaned, it felt like I was walking into the heat of a huge blow dryer. I found the tent for the military members who were on their way to Iraq and filled out the paperwork processing me into the Iraq theater. My arrival had now been documented in the U.S. government databases.

I found my way to the flight control tent and was manifested on a C-130 airplane which was heading to Anaconda and had room for a passenger. I boarded the C-130, donned my Kevlar helmet and ballistic eyeglasses, put on all my body armor, and waited as we entered the Iraq airspace.

Two hours later, we landed at Anaconda. Less than two weeks later, I was detailed as the lead defense counsel in *United States v. Sandoval.* Up until that moment in time, I had never given a great deal of thought to U.S. Army Field Manual 23-10 ("Sniper Training") or analyzed the defined mission of a sniper. That was all about to change.

THREE – CONFINEMENT PENDING TRIAL

"No person, while being held for trial, may be subjected to punishment or penalty other than arrest or confinement upon the charges pending against him, nor shall the arrest or confinement imposed upon him be any more rigorous than the circumstances required to ensure his presence…"

~ Article 13, Uniform Code of Military Justice

Like Sandoval, I too was surprised to discover that the military had a confinement facility in Kuwait. I didn't think there were enough U.S. military prisoners to fill a confinement facility given that the only people appropriate for confinement there would have had to fit very narrow criteria—be stationed in Kuwait, Afghanistan, or Iraq, be charged with a military crime, and be awaiting a court-martial or serving out a very short sentence.

Two weeks before traveling to FOB Iskan for the Article 32 hearing, I had flown to Kuwait to meet with Sandoval, introduce myself, and discuss the case with him. I was traveling with a fellow attorney who needed to go to Kuwait to meet with a client at a separate facility. I was happy to have a traveling companion who knew the lay of the land. This was extremely important as knowing how to get back to Balad from Kuwait was a skill in and of itself.

The confinement facility where Sandoval was being held was run by the U.S. Navy. The entire facility was comprised of a collection of tents and a couple of trailers surrounded by a big fence with concertina wire.[8] The most senior person on site was not a commissioned officer but a Chief Warrant Officer. So when I walked in as a Captain, I outranked the most senior person on site.

I stand six feet, two inches tall and had just gotten off the plane and walked through the desert heat from the air base to this facility as there were no TDS personnel with vehicles able to pick me up from the airfield and drive me around. I was tired, sweaty, caked in dust, and still wearing full combat gear. It was clear that I was coming directly from a combat zone, and I am sure I made quite an impression.

I entered the trailer, signed in, announced that I was there to see Specialist Sandoval, and surrendered my 9mm weapon. They addressed me as "Sir" and showed me all the deference one would expect to show the senior-ranking person on site.

They brought me into a small private room in the trailer and soon afterward, Sandoval was brought in. They had not put him in handcuffs but I did see something which was very disturbing: Sandoval was not wearing his rank. In the Army at that time, your rank was attached to the center of your uniform with Velcro material. Apparently, someone had decided to remove it.

Here was a soldier who had been convicted of nothing, and he wasn't even allowed the dignity of wearing his rank. As an Army Specialist, he was not a high-ranking individual, but he was nevertheless entitled to the rank, Specialist Sandoval. It was a dignity issue.

Further, removing Sandoval's rank from his uniform was in direct violation of Article 13 of the UCMJ, which provides that a person cannot be punished prior to conviction. Having

---

8   Concertina wire is barbed wire on large coils that are unrolled on the ground or on top of fences to serve as a military obstacle to protect an area from the enemy.

Sandoval in uniform yet preventing him from wearing his rank was essentially reducing him to the rank of Private—and any way you slice it, that is punishment and disrespectful to the soldier.

I was fuming and tempted to storm out and raise hell over it, but I decided to hold my tongue—for now. I would bring it up in due time, under the right circumstances and in the appropriate forum.

"Specialist Sandoval, my name is Captain Drummond," I said by way of introduction, "and I've been appointed as your attorney to represent you in this case. I recently deployed to Iraq from Fort Bliss, Texas, where I was working as a prosecutor. I've already read the limited information we have on the case. For me to properly defend you, it's also important for me to get to know you as a person and a soldier."

From reading the case file, I had expected to meet a large, imposing, arrogant soldier as he was assigned to an elite sniper unit in the most dangerous area of Iraq. What I instead found was a small but muscular man—one who appeared to be very, very stressed. Sandoval was respectful as he greeted me and told me a little bit about his life and military background. Right away I could see that he was a highly skilled warfighter, proud to be a soldier, but also was humble and sincere. His overriding feature was that he was confused and upset over what was going on.

He recounted being handcuffed and whisked away two weeks prior while on leave in Texas, then flown to the confinement facility in Kuwait. He told me that when he was arrested, he did not know what he had done wrong or what was going to happen with his case and future. Our meeting was his first opportunity to meet with an attorney to discuss his rights or the case.

"I'm afraid that during this first meeting I will have few

answers for you," I explained. "Mostly I'm here to introduce myself and outline the evidence in the case."

During that first meeting, I learned that Specialist Jorge G. Sandoval, Jr. was born in 1985 in Laredo, Texas, into a Hispanic-American family. Sandoval's father was an American citizen and his mother a Mexican national, and he had two older sisters, Norma and Sandra. During high school, he was active in Army Junior ROTC where he was in the Color Guard, served as a squad leader for his ROTC unit, and won numerous awards.

Upon graduation, he joined the Army as an 11Bravo— an Infantryman. He went to basic training and follow-on infantry training at Fort Benning, Georgia, where he learned how to be proficient with numerous firearms and prepare for combat. He was selected for Airborne School at Fort Benning and stayed three weeks, learning to jump out of C-130 aircraft. After earning his silver Airborne wings, he was assigned to the elite 501st Parachute Infantry Regiment out of Alaska in December of 2006. Sandoval was the first member of his family to join the Army.

"I want you to understand that I'm here for you," I said. "I only care about defending you."

"Thank you, sir. I honestly have no idea what's going on or why they are saying I'm a murderer."

"I am completely independent of your chain of command, and I don't give two shits about what your command wants. I don't give two shits about what crimes the prosecutors want to charge you with," I continued. "And I don't give two shits about what anybody wants but *you*. I'm here to fight for you. Now, for the Article 32 hearing, you will be flown back to FOB Iskan…"

"Oh, great! I miss my friends," he said. "It's been a long time since I've seen my squad."

During our conversation, Sandoval began to visibly relax.

As we talked, he came across as intelligent, but entirely new to the world of the military justice system.

I am not looking at a murderer, I was thinking to myself. *I am looking at a soldier, a young Airborne Infantry Paratrooper who we, the citizens of the United States, ordered into the most dangerous area in Iraq—the Triangle of Death!* The inherent danger of the region would be highlighted for me later when I requested access to visit the crime scene and was denied because it was "too dangerous."

"Now, once the Article 32 hearing is complete," I continued, "and all relevant evidence has been reviewed, the investigating officer will make a written recommendation to the commander who appointed him as to what should happen to the charges. He could recommend that all charges be dismissed or that you receive a reprimand or some other punishment or that the charges go forward to a general court-martial. However, his recommendation is non-binding in that the commander can still go forward to a general court-martial even if the investigating officer recommends dismissal."

The non-binding nature of the Article 32 causes some attorneys to consider the investigation to be a waste of time. I believe that such a perspective is shortsighted. The Article 32 serves as an important tool for both the government and the defense. For one thing, it provides the prosecutor and the command the ability to see any flaws in a weak case and provides a means of disposing of a case with flimsy evidence.

For example, the prosecutor can present the evidence in a less than zealous fashion and then give a weak explanation as to why the charges should go forward. Typically, if the prosecutor does not appear to be motivated about the case, then the investigating officer will likely recommend dismissal or lesser action than a court-martial such as a reprimand. In some cases, if the investigating officer recommends dismissal or light punishment, the chain of command then often agrees and disposes of the case with some minor punishment.

One of the most important functions of an Article 32 is to provide the prosecutor a means to gauge the sufficiency of evidence. For instance, if there is exculpatory evidence (evidence favorable toward the defendant) or evidence damaging to the government's case that is going to come out at trial, then it is important that the Investigating Officer hear it. This same evidence will be heard at trial by the panel, and if it shows a strong weakness in the case, there is often no sense wasting everyone's time with a trial.

Finally, if the case is weak and the investigating officer recommends not going to trial, then both justice and judicial economy weigh heavily in taking some other lesser action. The military justice system is positively unique in the respect that there are other options besides trial and conviction to deal with criminal misconduct whereas in almost all civilian criminal courts the options are guilty plea, trial, or dismissal. The options to reprimand someone, reduce them in rank, or kick them out of the Army via a separation board with an other than honorable (OTH) or general discharge are options available to commanders and are exercised in the vast majority of military cases, as opposed to proceeding with a court-martial.

After I had given Sandoval a sense of what to expect at the Article 32 hearing, he asked me to tell him about my background. There had apparently been a lot of discussion among the prisoners at the confinement facility on whether to hire civilian defense attorneys, who they perceived to be more experienced.

It was clear to me that Sandoval's family couldn't afford to hire a civilian attorney, and I wanted to reassure him that he was in good hands and not disadvantaged by having me represent him. I explained that I had previously been assigned as a military prosecutor and in that capacity, had prosecuted numerous serious crimes and taken many cases to trial, including a murder case. I was not being boisterous as the truth was that while I was at Fort Bliss it was expanding rapidly with an increase in soldiers, however the number of JAG lawyers assigned as prosecutors had not grown at the same pace. The result was that even though I was relatively young, I had already tried more major-felony level cases than most Judge Advocates do in their entire career. Sandoval was reassured to find out that I was an attorney who had dealt with major-felony cases and had experience in trial.

After I had reviewed the evidence in the case, I had the sense that the case against Sandoval was complete bullshit. After meeting and talking with him, that feeling was further reinforced. I had many questions related to his statement. Any time someone accused of a crime signs a statement, it is important to consider all the circumstances surrounding the preparing and signing of the statement. It's important, for example, to ascertain the age, education level, and alertness of the accused. I wanted to know whether Sandoval had carefully reviewed and signed the statement, if so, why he had signed it and whether he was tired at the time.

"Sir," he explained, "I was just trying to tell the truth. I don't think I did anything wrong!"

I would venture to say this was the most detailed and lengthy conversation Sandoval had ever had with an Army Captain, and I imagined it was probably intimidating for him. I was sure that prior to meeting me, he might have had, at most, a two-minute-long opportunity to sit with another Captain, his Company Commander—an officer in charge of at least one hundred soldiers.

I was thinking about how the very bedrock of the military is our vow to look out for our fellow soldiers. We never abandon a fallen comrade. Before we parted, I reiterated my intention to fight for him and said, "We're going to get through this together. You've got me for the long haul and now it is my turn to fight for you."

I felt very badly for Sandoval and more so after learning who he was to his family and his community. I thought about the fact that he was Army Junior ROTC in high school, he was also on the drill team and truly proud to serve our country. He had come from a family that was of humble means but honorable by all accounts. Sandoval was a smart man, a highly-trained Airborne Infantry Paratrooper and a combat-tested soldier. For all of this and for signing up to serve his country he was now facing a murder charge. I could not imagine what he was really thinking. I could only imagine that he felt he had let his family down and was betrayed by the county that he signed up to serve. The more I thought about the situation that the Army had put Sandoval in, the madder that I became.

I thought, *I'm truly all Sandoval has in this fight. If it were me, Mom and Dad would have been able to mortgage their house and potentially hire a team of attorneys come fight for me.* For Sandoval, he did not have significant financial resources or a team of attorneys. Instead, he only had me.

I felt lucky to have come from a family of modest financial success. Both of my parents came from large Catholic families with deep roots in the community; however, the similarities stop at that point. My father has four brothers and a sister, and my mother had five sisters and two now-deceased brothers. My father graduated from college, as had his father and grandfather, received his MBA, and became successful selling insurance to small businesses in St. Joseph. I consider my father's side of the family the formal side as they are all well-educated, financially successful people. My mother's family is made up of great hardworking people who represent all levels of the socioeconomic spectrum. I think of them as more informal considering that my mother was raised on a small dairy farm, was the first person ever in her family to attend college, and had to carry two full-time jobs in order to pay her way through school.

With this type of disparity among both sides of my family, I learned that money, or a successful appearance on the outside, doesn't make the person: you treat everyone with respect. This capacity to interact with diverse individuals regardless of their station in life has been a great asset in my work as an attorney. I believe it enables me to relate to different members of a jury without coming across as too cocky. I have no problem talking with a farmer about heifers and bailing hay, discussing trucks and tires with a trucker, or talking about the stock market and different mutual fund portfolios with a businessman. I credit my parents and both sides of their families with making sure that I was raised to be less judgmental than some of my peers in the legal community. I knew that winning this case was going to take more than just bravado and I hoped I could bring all of my background to assist in Sandoval's defense and his ultimate trial.

I stood up, shook Sandoval's hand and said, "Okay, see you in Iskan for the Article 32."

It was clear to me that Sandoval was guileless. He didn't believe he had done anything wrong and I didn't either. It was terrifying to think that my client was not guilty of the murder with which he had been charged. I walked away trying to wrap my head around the fact that the only one standing between him and Leavenworth prison was me. This enormous burden was now squarely on my shoulders.

FOUR – THE SNIPER SECTION

"When the need to integrate me into the sniper section arose, I saw it as an opportunity that fell into my lap, along with five other soldiers. It just so happened that our reconnaissance team was selected to be added to the sniper section. I thought, Yes, this may be very good experience for me. I am glad for the opportunity."

~ Specialist Jorge G. Sandoval, Jr.

Before heading to FOB Iskan, not only had I met with Sandoval but I had reviewed the case file. The investigation and case file up to that point had been generated by the CID Agents who had flown to the area weeks before, specifically to investigate three suspicious killings of Iraqis by U.S. soldiers.

There had been a two-week delay in releasing the case file to me as government prosecutors tried to determine what and how much of the case file itself was unclassified and suitable for release. When I finally received the file, it contained about twenty statements from witnesses, numerous pictures of the deceased, a couple of maps, notes, and reports. Some of the evidence was unclassified and other portions were classified and had to be retrieved on a special secure computer terminal and handled with caution.

Not only was Sandoval charged with murder and with wrongfully planting evidence with the remains of the deceased on 27 April, charges had been filed against another sniper in Sandoval's unit, specifically Staff Sergeant (SSG) Michael Hensley for an event on 11 May 2007. As such the case file also contained statements and evidence related to those charges. Sergeant (SGT) Evan Vela, a third member of

Sandoval's unit, was charged with the incident of 11 May. Sandoval would also later be charged with crimes related to that subsequent incident.

As I read through the case file, the theory of the government's case became clear. The events surrounding the charges occurred on 27 April 2007 in the rural farmland area on the outskirts of the city of Iskandariyah, an area consisting primarily of flooded fields and marshlands bordering the Euphrates River.

The area was routinely patrolled by Sandoval's unit, the 501st Parachute Infantry Regiment based out of Fort Richardson, Alaska. The unit had deployed to the area in September 2006 and was comprised of about 350 soldiers. The 501st had both light infantry and sniper elements assigned to it.

"There were a handful of us in the unit who were not school-trained snipers," explained Sandoval. "We were integrated into the sniper section by experienced members of the section. They were in charge of us and had trained us over a three- to four-week period in Iraq."

On 27 April, Sandoval was on a sniper patrol in a rural farmland area with his sniper unit. The other members of his unit with him were Hensley (the sniper section leader and senior soldier in the unit); Sergeant (SGT) Anthony Murphy (a fellow sniper); and Specialist (SPC) Alexander Flores (another fellow sniper).

The 27th was the third day of a three-day mission, and all the members of the unit were tired and ready to return to FOB Iskan. At some point that morning, a majority of the snipers were gathered and somewhat camouflaged in a field of high grass, resting, pulling security, and eating.

Flores was on a high area of ground and was the first to observe an Iraqi man cutting grass about 300 meters away. Within a few minutes, all the snipers had their eyes trained on the man. According to Flores, the man was not doing anything out of the ordinary.

According to the prosecution, as the morning dragged on and Hensley watched the man cutting grass in the field, he decided that he would kill the man for no real reason. Hensley made visual contact with Sandoval and directed him to follow him away from the others. They both low-crawled through the high grass toward the man. Hensley and Sandoval got into shooting positions, lying down with their sniper rifles pointed at the man.

A few minutes later, Hensley asked Sandoval if he had the shot.

Sandoval immediately fired and hit the man squarely in the head. The impact of the round ripped most of the man's head in half, killing him instantly.

According to the prosecution, Hensley and Sandoval quickly approached the body. Once there, Hensley ordered Sandoval to place command wire on the man's body.

Sandoval complied. The wire was presumably placed on the body to make it appear the deceased man was an insurgent involved with planting IEDs.

That was the government's theory.

A few days prior to Sandoval's removal from his mother's house by CID Agents on 26 June 2007, Sandoval's life took a dramatic turn, although he was completely unaware of it. Around 22 June 2007, two soldiers had been reprimanded for minor disciplinary infractions on the FOB. In response to being punished, they told their chain of command that they had overheard Hensley, Sandoval, and other soldiers talking about shootings that they did not feel were justified. The soldiers also reported seeing enemy weapons and ammunition in the possession of Hensley and others that should have been reported and turned in to the command.

CID immediately opened an investigation into a number

of the unit's recent shootings as well as the unauthorized weapons, and it was that investigation which led the agents to arrest Sandoval in Laredo, Texas, on 26 June 2007.

Following the two-hour interrogation of Sandoval conducted by CID Agents at the local Laredo police station, the agents had typed up a statement, and Sandoval had signed it. In the statement, Sandoval stated that at the time of the shot, all he could see was "the head of the individual" and that he did not see a weapon on the man.

Sandoval stated that Hensley had directed the shot and admitted that "Hensley gave me command wire...I laid the wire next to the body."

◆ ◆ ◆

SPECIALIST JORGE G. SANDOVAL, JR.

Sandoval stated in his sworn statement to CID as follows:

On 27 April 2007, my sniper team, which consisted of two heavy teams and one bolt team, were supposed to do a mortar interdiction mission. On the 27th, we got the call the adjacent teams were moving up route Lorrie. While the adjacent team was en route, we heard machine gun fire. The MiTT Team[9] got a call from MOHAWK 6, LT Matthew Didier, who stated the Iraqi Army was in contact with Army insurgents.

We then started to move back south, and SSG Hensley got a call from someone on the heavy team and stated someone was moving in our direction and this coincided with what LT Didier had said. It was not too long afterward that we saw a

---

9 A MiTT team, or military transition team, is an element of U.S. soldiers embedded within an Iraqi unit. The MiTT teams, eat, sleep, and fight alongside the Iraqis. The mission of MiTT teams is to make Iraqi Army units self-sustainable tactically, operationally and logistically so that the unit is prepared to take over responsibility of certain geographic areas.

guy walking and then he popped a squat. We got in place at which time I could only see the head of the individual. SSG Hensley asked if I had the shot.

I said, "No."

SSG Hensley says again, "Do you have it now?"

I said no again.

SSG Hensley then asks again, "How about now?"

I told him, "I got it." I pulled the trigger. I then picked up and moved to the body. I drew my 9mm, and then put it back into its holster. SSG Hensley gave me command wire. I laid the wire next to the body. We then went back to the hole. Some of the other guys had to go conduct Sensitive Site Exploitation. I didn't want to go. We all then consolidated and we had to hump the body out.

SPC Josh Michaud carried the body about 200 meters south, where it was picked up by the Apache. Then we moved out.

Then on the 11th of May, SGT Vela killed an Iraqi man. On the day this happened, I and SGT Robert Redfern were in the pump house when SGT Vela shot the Iraqi national. SGT Vela was with SSG Hensley and SGT Rich Hand. I know that an AK-47 was planted on the Iraqi national's body. That is all I know about this incident.

After the narrative portion of the statement there was a written question and answer portion as follows:

(Q: SPECIAL AGENT WOODCOX)

(A: SPC SANDOVAL)

Q: On 27 April, where did you get the command wire you placed on the Iraqi national?

A: From SSG Hensley.

Q: Where did SSG Hensley get the command wire from?

A: I don't know. He handed it to me and said, "Here you go."

Q: Did SSG Hensley tell you to place the command wire on the body of the Iraqi?

A: Yes.

Q: Did you see any visual confirmation to take the shot from anyone besides SSG Hensley?

A: No.

Q: Did SSG Hensley tell you to shoot the Iraqi national?

A: Yes.

Q: What is command wire?

A: Thin wire used by insurgents to employ IEDs.

Q: Were there any other weapons found on or around the Iraqi national you shot on 27 April?

A: No.

Q: Were there any indications on the Iraqi national you shot on 27 April that he had a weapon or shot a weapon?

A: Not that I could tell.

Q: When you arrived to the location, what did it appear the Iraqi national was doing when you saw him?

A: That he was hiding.

Q: How can you tell that he was hiding if all you could see was his head?

A: As we maneuvered, I could see him pop a squat.

Q: What does the Rules of Engagement say about engaging targets?

A: Hostile act or hostile intent.

Q: Was there a hostile act or hostile intent displayed by the Iraqi national you shot on 27 April?

A: No.

Q: When the SSE[10] was conducted, what was found on the body of the Iraqi national?

A: The command wire I placed on the right side of the body.

Q: Did you place the command wire on or by the Iraqi national you shot on the 27th of April?

A: Yes.

Q: Prior to you placing the command wire on the Iraqi national, did you find any command wire on the Iraqi national you shot on the 27th of April?

A: No.

Q: Did you place an AK-47 on the Iraqi national that was shot by SGT Vela?

A: No.

Q: Was there an AK-47 found on or by the Iraqi National shot by SGT Vela?

A: Yes.

Q: Do you know who placed the AK-47 on the Iraqi national shot by SGT Vela?

A: No.

Q; How do you know about the AK-47 being placed on the Iraqi national shot by SGT Vela?

A: I heard someone mumble something about, "Who's got the AK-47?" This was some time on 10 May 07,

---

10   SSE, or Sensitive Site Exploitation, is the common term for cataloging a kill or recording details about a certain location, such as a weapons cache. It generally consists of photographing the body or area and retrieving any important evidence. Normally there are special SSE teams set up for this specific purpose, however it was not uncommon in Iraq for the unit on the ground to initially catalog a kill and record the pertinent information.

about 2300.

Q: Who did you hear mumble about the AK-47?

A: I'm not sure who it was.

Q: Who was there with you when you heard the conversation about the AK-47?

A: SSG Hensley, SGT Hand, SGT Vela, and SGT Redfern.

Q: Where would you find an AK-47 to place on the body?

A: I don't know.

Q: Do you know why someone would say you placed an AK-47 on the Iraqi national?

A: No.

Q: Has SSG Hensley shot or given the order to shoot an Iraqi national while you were present besides on the 11th of May 2007 and 27th of Apr 2007?

A: No.

Q: Do you believe SSG Hensley received the green light to shoot an unarmed Iraqi national?

A: Yes, on 27 April 2007.

Q: Do you know it is in violation of U.S. Customs and Laws to shoot an unarmed local national?

A: Yes.

Q: Have you ever shot at other Iraqi nationals after being ordered by SSG Hensley?

A: No.

Q: How have you been treated this afternoon?

A: Fine.

Q: Were you afforded opportunities for food, drinks, and bathroom breaks?

A: Yes.

Q: Is there anything else you'd like to add to this?

A: No.

(Statement taken at the Laredo Police Department, Laredo Texas 26 June 2007)

♦♦♦

In the military, generally following an order is an absolute defense to a crime. However, if the order was unlawful and the person following the order should have known it was unlawful, then the defense does not apply. Typically, for a person to be a legitimate target on a battlefield, that person must have engaged in a hostile act or demonstrate hostile intent towards U.S. or coalition forces. If no hostile act or hostile intent, then there is no legitimate target.

The government's theory seemed to be that if the man was unarmed and Sandoval did not directly see the man engage in a hostile act toward him or others, then the shooting was not lawful or justified and was therefore murder, regardless if the shooting was ordered by SSG Hensley.

"While I was in confinement," Sandoval would later recall, "I had a lot of time to reflect. Despite my imprisonment and the charges being brought against me, I didn't really see how I could have done anything differently. I never had any reason to doubt anyone in my platoon or my section. I had been with that platoon for quite some time by the spring of 2007 and knew all these guys to be standup guys. SSG Hensley was a very well-respected soldier and leader within our battalion. So I trusted the man. And it may sound strange, but I trust him to this day."

♦♦♦

The government had its case and had its alleged

confession. They were proceeding on the theory that Hensley had ordered Sandoval to shoot an innocent farmer cutting grass and Sandoval complied. At first glance, it appeared to be a lock-tight case for the prosecution.

By the time I was detailed to the case, it had already made headlines in numerous newspapers, including the *Stars and Stripes*. The Army Public Affairs Office in Baghdad had issued a press release about the multiple deaths and subsequent charges in Iskandariyah, stating "Soldiers Charged with Premeditated Murder," which detailed the charges against Sandoval and Hensley.

Hensley was also charged with two other murders and a number of related crimes. The civilian newspapers who reported on the press release made it appear that the charges were straightforward and the shootings were murders.

For the charges, Sandoval faced a maximum punishment of life without the possibility of parole. Literally his freedom and his life were going to come down to the disposition of his case. I knew that I had my work cut out for me. Being assigned to defend a soldier charged with murder was one of the biggest challenges that I had ever faced.

FIVE - THE ARTICLE
32 INVESTIGATION

"No charge or specification may be referred to a general court-martial for trial until a thorough and impartial investigation of all the matters set forth therein has been made."

~ Article 32, Uniform Code of Military Justice

The case was advancing lightning fast toward trial. I learned that the prosecutors were moving forward quickly as they wanted to get the case to trial in Iraq before Sandoval's unit re-deployed (left the combat zone to return to its home station of Alaska) in November of 2007.

The next step in moving the case forward was conducting the Article 32 hearing.[11] Some Article 32 hearings are a simple bump in the road for the prosecution where the investigating officer recommends going forward with the charges regardless of how the evidence plays out. Other investigating officers truly examine all the evidence with the required skepticism and perhaps recommend dismissal of some or all the charges, or possibly a disposition to a level lower than a general court-martial.

With all the unknowns, the Article 32 poses a number of issues for the defense counsel. It is a great opportunity to learn about the case, to assess witness testimony and to

---

11   After the events in this case, Congress enacted significant changes to the Article 32 process in the *National Defense Authorization Act for Fiscal Year 2014*. Some of these changes limit an accused's rights at the Article 32 and changed the name of the procedure to "pretrial hearings." This book is focusing solely on the Article 32 process as it existed in 2007 during the case and trial of SPC Sandoval. The same process discussed in this book is the same process that was in existence for essentially the sixty years before the changes in 2014.

understand the government's theory of the case. However, the positive aspects have to be weighed against the negative because the prosecution can learn the same key information about the defense's case if the defense puts on all its evidence at the Article 32 investigation instead of waiting for trial. If the defense lays out detailed evidence and pulls out all its zingers on cross-examination, then it has also just shown its hand as to how the defense case will play out at trial.

Based on these pitfalls, some defense attorneys decide against offering any evidence at the Article 32 and merely sit back and listen. The do-nothing approach is sometimes wise because that way the prosecutor and government investigators have no idea at the time of trial where the defense is heading in regard to their theory and cross-examination of witnesses. In that sense, the government is not sure how the trial will go and oftentimes may be unprepared for a certain theory of defense or a cross-examination of certain witnesses, thus giving the defense potential advantages. In civilian courts, where discovery is often very limited by the rules and by the judges, this is a common approach in defense of a case.

However, given the requirements that the defense attorneys in military cases disclose so much of their case in pretrial disclosures, this approach is not typically the best one to take at an Article 32. This is especially true where the government is ill-prepared for the Article 32 and the defense attorneys can lock down witnesses to certain versions of events during their sworn testimony.

Just like any trial, civilian or military, there are tons of questions and tons of strategic decisions made about how to proceed. A trial is very much like surgery in that you must take big steps to move forward but even a small mistake can kill the case. The key to an effective strategy for an Article 32 is to remember that in the end, the investigating officer is simply making a recommendation.

At the time of the Article 32 for Sandoval, I was aware of

recent news reports that murder charges against two Marines in the media-popular Haditha killings had been dismissed by their Commanding General after the Article 32 investigating officer recommended not going forward.

Haditha was perhaps one of the worst war crimes committed by U.S. Marines. On 19 November 2005 in the city of Haditha, Iraq, twenty-four Iraqi men, women, and children were killed by U.S. Marines. It was alleged that the killings were without direct provocation and instead were retribution for an attack on a convoy of Marines where one was killed. One sergeant was alleged to have ordered his men to "shoot first and ask questions later." The killings were widely reported in the media and several Marines were originally charged with crimes related to the killings. During the course of their Article 32 investigation, much of the testimony was contradictory and, as such, charges against some of the Marines were dropped altogether by their Commanding General.

◆ ◆ ◆

Although one Marine General's implementation of military justice by dismissing charges is not a good benchmark for what an Army General would do, I was aware that there was the possibility that dismissal could happen with Sandoval's murder charge as well. Given that Sandoval was sitting in confinement awaiting trial, I decided to take a chance and zealously attack the evidence at the Article 32. There was a possibility that the investigating officer would see the ridiculousness of the charges. I thought that it would be best to go ahead and expose some of our defense case if the benefit resulted in the dismissal of the most serious charge—murder—or at the very least Sandoval's release from confinement while awaiting trial.

When I flew to the location of the Article 32, I did not know what to expect. FOB Iskan was remote, small, and located in the same compound as the Musayyib power plant. This massive, dirty plant powered by crude oil provided electricity for nearly twenty-five percent of Iraq. The smoke that the plant churned out through its four massive smokestacks coated everything as it settled among the buildings and military compound below. The U.S.-occupied buildings at FOB Iskan were within a few hundred meters of the smokestacks and within walking distance of the power plant—not a pleasant place to be.

The Article 32 took place inside a large Saddam-era warehouse that the 501st had turned into their battalion headquarters. The U.S. troops had sectioned off the main area of the warehouse and built plywood offices and room dividers. The largest room was the battalion's conference room which was designated as the location for the investigation.

The charges against Sandoval and the charges against Hensley were consolidated into one Article 32 investigation and hearing. The prosecutors had originally planned on having an even larger consolidated investigation by having the charges against Vela investigated at the same time. As it turned out, Vela's defense attorney was stateside on deployment leave and had to delay his hearing. With Vela's attorney gone, the prosecutors made the decision to move forward with the investigation against just Sandoval and Hensley.

When we were initially notified that the Article 32 was also going to involve Hensley, we made the strategic decision not to object to the consolidation as it would give us the opportunity to view all the evidence against both Sandoval and Hensley. As it appeared that Hensley had directed the shooting of 27 April, we wanted to know as much about him and all of his charges as possible.

I traveled to the hearing with my immediate supervisor, senior defense counsel, Captain (CPT) Yolanda McCray, who was not only going to be assisting me at the hearing but also interviewing witnesses. As she was the most senior attorney in my office, her assistance was greatly welcomed. It was our understanding that government prosecutors had not been there before our arrival, so neither the witnesses nor the leadership of the accused soldiers had been interviewed by attorneys on either side. This was a huge strategic advantage for the preparation and defense of our case as it allowed us to be the first ones to give the witnesses our perspective and opinions of the charges and the case.

The Brigade Commander for Sandoval and Hensley appointed Major (MAJ) Oliver Hasse as the investigating officer, and he had flown into Iskandariyah the previous day. During the period of time in which Sandoval faced these charges, the general practice of military commanders was to assign the role of investigating officer in an Article 32 to regular, non-attorney military officers.

I knew very little about Hasse other than the fact that he was stationed on a large U.S. compound located on the outskirts of Baghdad and was a staff officer with the 3rd Infantry Division who coordinated air support flights for the Division Level Command in the normal course of his job. His usual work duties did not entail anything that could be construed as investigative or related to military justice issues, so I found his appointment curious given the complex and serious nature of the charges.

◆ ◆ ◆

The room was cold and loud. The walls of the conference room were newly built with a single layer of plywood. With plywood as the only barrier between the room and the rest of the drafty warehouse, it was less of a room and more like a freestanding shack that could blow over with a large gust of wind. The large portable air conditioning units grumbled as they tried to keep the air at 85 degrees F. Along the wall there were photos of the members of Sandoval's unit who had lost their lives in Iraq. Someone had the idea to place a sheet of paper over their faces in an apparent effort to mask the fact that we were in a war-zone investigating shootings by the same unit who were also taking their own casualties from the enemy.

As the evidence was examined for the first time and the witnesses cross-examined, it became clear that the relevant timeline of the shooting did not start when Hensley first spotted the insurgent cutting grass. Rather the timeline began half an hour before the shooting when the Iraqi Army and U.S. forces were attacked by insurgents 1,000 meters to the southwest of Hensley and Sandoval's location.

A number of witnesses explained that the farmlands on the outskirts of Iskandariyah were a very dangerous place where the main roads were lined with improvised explosive devices (IEDs) and that while on patrol in that area, U.S. troops were certain to come under attack. The reason that Hensley, Sandoval and other U.S. soldiers were in the farmlands on that day was because they were on a counter-mortar mission to find and kill insurgents emplacing mortars[12] and shooting at FOB Iskan or other U.S. and Iraqi Army soldiers on patrols.

As one soldier testified about the mission, "The purpose of our mission was to try and locate and identify the mortar point-of-origin site and identify any anti-Iraqi forces individuals loosing[13] mortar rounds against coalition forces and to interdict the anti-Iraqi forces."

It also became abundantly clear that the man that Sandoval shot was not a farmer simply cutting grass. The pictures in the evidence file of the man Sandoval shot that

---

12   "Emplacing mortars" is the term for setting up the mortar launching stand and aiming the mortar round in the direction you want it to travel.

13   "Loosing" is an informal term used by members of the artillery for releasing and launching rockets or mortars into the air.

morning depicted a deceased male wearing a black long-sleeve shirt and dark blue pants. The testimony made clear that this was not the outfit of an indigenous Iraqi farmer nor of most men in the area, who typically wore an ankle-length, robe-like garment called a dishdasha.[14] Given that the dishdasha is made from cotton with an open bottom for the garment to breathe, it was the preferred dress of the Iraqi farmer in the fields.

The importance of the clothing the deceased was wearing became evident during the testimony of Captain (CPT) Matthew Didier (who had recently been promoted from First Lieutenant). Didier was Hensley and Sandoval's platoon leader and the senior U.S. Army officer on the ground on 27 April. He had been out on patrol that morning with a MiTT team. This particular MiTT team patrolled the geographic area of Iskandariyah and often conducted missions in coordination with Sandoval's unit.

◆ ◆ ◆

CAPTAIN MATTHEW DIDIER

CPT Didier testified on direct examination from the prosecutor at the Article 32, as follows:

(Q: PROSECUTOR)

(A: CPT DIDIER)

Q: Where were you on 27 April 2007?

A: 27 April? I was patrolling with the MiTT team, U.S. soldiers and the Iraqi Army up in the "fish farm" area.

Q: And what were you doing with the MiTT and the Iraqi Army?

A: We were going to investigate a cache site that Staff Sergeant Hensley and the snipers had identified the

---

14   U.S. forces commonly referred to the dishdasha as a "man dress."

night prior as a possible cache site. We were going to investigate if there were any weapons or anything there.

Q: Did you have any contact while you were out there?

A: Yes, the Iraqi Army made contact about 100 meters just north of fish farm 3, on the west side of Route Lima with two individuals. They broke contact moving north/northeast from our location. The MiTT team gave me a description of dark clothing, not man-dresses, more like running suits or track suits that they were wearing, and said that they were breaking contact north/northeast from our position, which would lead them toward our snipers.

Q: So what did you do upon receiving that information?

A: I called Staff Sergeant Hensley and gave him the description of two individuals and the direction they were coming from.

Q: Did anything happen after that?

A: About 10 to 15 minutes later, he called me on the net to let me know that he had eyes on two individuals that fit that description crossing Route Lima.

Q: And did you hear any further radio contact from him?

A: About 10 to 15 minutes after that, he told me that he got eyes on one of the individuals coming out, moving east away from Route Lima to a clearing. He asked me if he had permission to engage that individual. I said, "Are you sure it's one of the guys you'd seen go in there?" He said, "Roger." And I gave him permission.

Q: And you authorized it based on the description of what was happening and what he saw?

A: Yes, ma'am.

Q: You yourself were not there?

A: No, ma'am.

Q: Did Staff Sergeant Hensley tell you how far away this individual was that he had eyes on?

A: About 100 to 200 meters away.

Q: Did you consider the distance somehow when you gave him permission based on the distance? Was there some thinking that you did as far as how far away he was?

A: A little bit, ma'am, not a lot. Because he was a small element out there on his own.

Q: Did you think that that individual was far enough away that he would have the ability to get away if he wasn't shot?

A: Yes, ma'am...

At that point, I was uncertain as to where the prosecutor was going with her questions. She was confirming that Captain Didier had given the order to engage and that the order was to kill someone who had attacked the MiTT team. Didier's testimony continued for over two hours.

After lengthy questioning, I ended my cross-examination with Didier as follows:

Q: Again, they confirmed with you that "squirters"[15] running from an engagement, even if they don't have a weapon, if they're not surrendering or giving up when

---

15   A "squirter" is military lingo for a person, most likely the enemy, fleeing from a military attack.

they have PID[16], you can engage?"

A: Yes.

Q: How many soldiers have been lost or killed in this area, in the area of FOB Iskandariyah since you've been here?

A: 15 to 20.

Q: Pretty dangerous place?

A: At times it can be, yes.

The most intriguing element about Didier's testimony was that it had not been captured in any of the sworn statements made by Army investigators before the Article 32. Didier had made a typewritten sworn statement and nowhere in it was he asked if he ordered the shooting and nowhere in it did he volunteer that he ordered the shooting. To be clear, Didier had just testified that he ordered the shooting of 27 April and that the person Sandoval shot was the enemy, someone who had just attacked the Iraqi Army and was fleeing in the direction of Sandoval and Hensley.

◆ ◆ ◆

The second major surprise of the investigation came during the testimony of SPC Flores, another sniper who had been out with Sandoval and Hensley on the morning of the 27th. According to his sworn statement, he had been crouched near a canal about 200 meters from Sandoval. In Flores' written statement to the CID, he stated that he saw the man who Sandoval shot cutting grass that morning, thus

---

16   PID is defined as positive identification where a soldier identifies a hostile target. The question might be posed to a soldier, "Do you have PID?" They are being asked whether they can positively identify that an individual is a hostile target based upon their uniform, firearms, actions, etc.

supporting the prosecutor's position that the man posed no threat.

SPECIALIST ALEXANDER THOMAS FLORES

SPC Flores stated in his sworn statement of 22 June 2007, as follows:

On the third day in the morning, a man came out to the field and began cutting grass with a small sickle-like tool. We watched him for a while that morning and the only behavior we saw was him cutting grass. I didn't see any other weapons or tools on him. At some point, the man left the field. I went to sleep for a few hours and when I awoke, I noticed the man had returned and walked back to the same spot he was at and started cutting grass again. I started to watch him through a set of binoculars.

SSG Hensley told SPC Sandoval to grab his rifle because they were going to take the guy out. SSG Hensley grabbed his rifle and they headed out to maneuver around the man cutting grass about 150 meters south of my location. I was switching, watching both SSG Hensley and SPC Sandoval maneuver around the man and watching the man continue to cut the grass. As SSG Hensley and SPC Sandoval approached the man, he watched them approach but kept cutting the grass. SPC Sandoval took the shot and hit the man with one shot in the front of the head…

The government's alleged timeline regarding Flores' involvement was that the insurgent was shot, and then Sandoval and Hensley went out to the body, and Sandoval placed detonation wire in the man's pocket. They then returned and pulled security, guarding them from any hostile forces that may have heard the shot, and then radioed in the kill. Sometime thereafter, Hensley and Flores went out to the body and Flores took pictures of the detonation wire on the deceased's body.

The Flores' statements were damning evidence and supported the prosecution's theory that Sandoval had placed detonation wire on the deceased body to cover up the kill— because it was an illegal kill and he knew it.

To everyone's surprise, including the prosecutor asking the questions, at the Article 32 when Flores was asked about his actions after he heard the shot from Sandoval's rifle, he testified as follows:

(Q: PROSECUTOR)

(A: SPC FLORES)

"Q: Okay. Did you stay after the shot? Did you stay sitting in the canal?

A: Yes, I did.

Q: At some point did you go up to the body?

A: At some point, yes, I did.

Q: About how long after the shot did you go up to the body?

A: Maybe about 15 or 20 minutes?

Q: Why?

A: To take pictures.

Q: Did someone tell you to go up to the body and take pictures?

A: Yes.

Q: Who was that?

A: Staff Sergeant Hensley.

Q: Do you always bring your camera with you on missions?

A: Most of the time, yes, I do.

Q: What do you use your camera for?

A: I use my camera in order to take just SSE (Sensitive Site Exploitation) pictures and stuff like that. I've used my camera before in the same situation.

Q: Did Staff Sergeant Hensley tell you when you went up to the body with your camera, did he also tell you to bring anything else?

A: Yes.

Q: What did he say?

A: He told me to grab the spool of wire and put it in my pocket.

Q: What kind of wire?

A: Just command wire. A small spool.

Q: Did you have command wire with you, to your knowledge, at that point?

A: No, I didn't have the command wire on me.

Q: Did you look around at all when he said to bring the command wire?

A: Yes, I did.

Q: Did you then see command wire?

A: Yes, I did.

Q: Where did you see it?

A: I saw it on top of my rucksack.

Q: What did you do when you saw the wire?

A: I grabbed the wire and I put it in my left cargo pocket.

Q: And then what did you do?

A: I got my camera and grabbed my weapon and I got up and walked over to the body.

Q: Did you go over to the body with anybody else?

A: Yes.

Q: Who?

A: Staff Sergeant Hensley.

Q: Was there anybody else?

A: No, it was just us two.

Q: What did you do when you went up to the body then?

A: I went up to the body and just examined it for a little bit. And then he told me to just get my camera ready to take pictures.

Q: And did you take pictures?

A: Yes, I did.

Q: Of what?

A: Of the body.

Q: With the command wire?

A: Yes.

Q: Did Staff Sergeant Hensley talk to you about why he wanted you to place the command wire on the body?

A: No, he didn't.

Q: And did it occur to you to question why he wanted you to place the wire on the body?

A: No, it didn't occur to me to question it.

Q: Why not?

A: I don't know.

Q: And did you do anything with the wire after you were done with the pictures?

A: Yes, I did. I put it back in my pocket."

◆ ◆ ◆

Thus, according to Flores, it was *he* who had placed the wire on the body and photographed it. This was consistent with Flores' statements as captured in his sworn statement to the CID (the first half of which is quoted above and the second half of which follows here):

…They returned to our position. SSG Hensley needed another soldier to check the body even after the platoon leader told him to stay at his position until the platoon leader arrived. SSG Hensley blew the platoon leader off and took SPC Michaud and SPC Haulotte with him to check the body. SPC Sandoval was too freaked out about the shoot to go see the body. They just looked at the body but didn't touch it for a few minutes.

Then they came back to our position and he asked me if I had my camera and I told him I did. SSG Hensley told someone to give me the roll of command wire. I took the wire and put it in my pocket and walked over to the body with SSG Hensley, took a couple of pictures of SSG Hensley and the body and then SSG Hensley told me to put the command wire in the man's light pants pocket. Then I took a couple more pictures of the body and took a couple of pictures of the guy's head and then walked back to our position…

Sandoval had stated in his sworn statement made before the investigation and before he was detailed a defense attorney that *he* had placed the wire on the body, as follows:

I pulled the trigger. I then picked up and moved to the body. I drew my 9mm, and then put it back into its holster. SSG Hensley gave me command wire. I laid the wire next to the body. We then went back to the hole. Some of the other guys had to go conduct Sensitive Site Exploitation. I didn't want to go…

What was the misunderstanding? There were some clear

contradictions between Flores' and Sandoval's statements about placing the command wire on the deceased's body. These were glaring inconsistencies. Why were two soldiers seemingly admitting to the same crime?

At the time, I was uncertain but at a minimum I thought this raised reasonable doubt as to what actually happened on the day in question and who did what. If Flores was going to be a government witness to support the theory that the deceased was merely cutting grass, then he was also going to cut a striking blow to the government's theory when he would testify that it was he who had placed wire on the body and photographed it.

SIX - THE SNIPER
FIELD MANUAL

"Each member of the sniper team has specific responsibilities... The observer selects an appropriate target..."

"Sniper Training," U.S. Army
Field Manual 23-10 (1994)

The developing argument against the government's case was this: even if Sandoval had made the wrong call by shooting the deceased, the call was not his to make. The sniper team is comprised of both a shooter and an observer, and the United States Army Field Manual 23-10 ("Sniper Training") directs that each member of the sniper team has specific responsibilities and that selecting the appropriate target is the observer's call. The Army's own manual on snipers puts the call to shoot on the observer and not the shooter.

It goes on: "The primary mission of a sniper in combat is to support combat operations by delivering precise long-range fire on selected targets. By this, the sniper creates casualties among enemy troops, slows enemy movement, frightens enemy soldiers, lowers morale, and adds confusion to their operations." (Army Field Manual 23-10 §1-1)

During the Article 32, I introduced the Army Field Manual 23-10 into evidence and questioned another sniper in Sandoval's unit about sniper tactics. This sniper, Specialist (SPC) Hugo Castro Barragan, was formally trained at the Sniper School at Fort Benning, Georgia, had extensive combat experience, had nothing to do with any of the charges, and was not under investigation. The importance of having his testimony was to point out on the record that Hensley's actions that morning in being the observer and relaying to

Sandoval that there was a shot, that there was a kill to make, places the decision of whether the deceased was a legitimate target on Hensley and not Sandoval.

Barragan explained how to apply to real life and real combat the guidance outlined in the Army Field Manual 23-10, as follows:

(Q: DEFENSE COUNSEL)

(A: SPC BARRAGAN)

Q: Specialist, if the observer and shooter are laying down side by side, that's a somewhat normal position for snipers, is that correct?

A: Yes, it is.

Q: And if the observer is looking at the target and the observer is determining if it's an appropriate target, the observer begins to relay to the shooter, "Hey, do you have the shot? Do you have the kill?" That's also relaying to that shooter that that's an appropriate target to take out, correct?

A: Yes, sir.

After I concluded, the investigating officer was visually perplexed and asked the sniper for further clarification, as follows:

Investigating officer: So to clarify what Captain Drummond said, it was Staff Sergeant Hensley's call, based off the situation from the moving enemy to the grass location. The fact that Captain Didier said to engage people coming from the east. According to the Rules of Engagement, Staff Sergeant Hensley allowed Specialist Sandoval to engage. At least that's how it would come down based off of crew-coordination that was explained to me earlier?

Barragan: I guess if that's what Captain Didier said, coming from the east, you know…

Q: Okay, right, I understand you don't know if he did

say that.

The investigating officer then turned to me and asked, "I believe that is what you are trying to put all together for me?"

"Yes, sir. Showing that the sniper regulation and the sniper training puts the call on the observer," I replied.

The investigating officer then nodded and said, "It's a crew coordination and just like in a vehicle, the tank commander makes the decision on whether the vehicle goes right or left, the driver just executes the movement of that vehicle."

♦ ♦ ♦

While the Article 32 proceeding, itself was valuable, as I was able to see and hear the evidence presented for the first time, the most important information I learned was through my own investigation outside of the event, meeting with witnesses and reviewing evidence that the government had not presented during the Article 32.

In talking with Didier outside of the Article 32, he said that an Iraqi Army officer who was working with U.S. troops identified the body of the deceased as an insurgent—the enemy. Didier also said that the officer may be located a short distance from FOB Iskan. CPT McCray and I then went to the battalion Tactical Operations Center (TOC)[17] to see if we could go out to meet the Iraqi officer. We were told that he was located with a U.S. Army MiTT team close to FOB Iskan and that they could coordinate a meeting.

On the evening of 23 July 2007 after the Article 32 had recessed for the day, McCray and I ventured outside of

17   A Tactical Operations Center, or TOC, is a unit's command post where most radio traffic is monitored, enemy positions targeted, and coordination between friendly units in the area is controlled. It is the operational command center for the unit.

the relative security of the base's gates to the Iraqi Army compound. To say we "ventured outside" is perhaps a mischaracterization of what actually occurred. Since we did not have our own vehicle, we originally asked to be driven to the Iraqi compound in an armored vehicle, and this was denied by Sandoval's leadership at FOB Iskan. We were lawyers and trained Army officers, but we carried only 9mm side arms and were by no means a heavily armed combat team. Other than knowing that we were in the Triangle of Death—one of the most dangerous areas in the world at the time—we knew nothing about how dangerous the road was between FOB Iskan and the Iraqi Army compound.

We had no idea exactly where we were going "down the road." In fact, it was unclear how far down the road the compound even was. When we asked for clarification, one of the operations officers sitting in the comfort of the TOC just kept smirking and mentioning that it was "not far." Nonetheless, believing that it was our job as Sandoval's defense team to gather as much information as possible about the case and potential witnesses, with no vehicles, no combat support, and only two 9mm handguns between us, we watched the large armored gate open, and we walked out of FOB Iskan onto the road leading away from the relative safety of the compound.

One of the guards mounted in a security tower with a 50mm machine gun guarding the base yelled down a password for us to say when we returned. "Scared shitless" does not accurately describe our venture "down the road" that night to the Iraqi compound. Thankfully, the compound was less than half a mile away, and we were not attacked as we walked briskly along the road.

Even though the TOC had earlier radioed that we were on our way and when we arrived it was clear that they were expecting us, we were still met with questioning glances by all the Iraqi soldiers. Two Iraqi soldiers led us inside to a large room where we sat down on a stained and dilapidated couch.

Captain (CPT) Douglas Mulvaney, a U.S. Army officer and intelligence advisor for the MiTT team, entered, introduced himself, and asked how he could be of assistance. We explained that we were looking for the Iraqi officer who had identified the body on 27 April. CPT Mulvaney was immediately familiar with the identification and the events of that day. In fact, he said that he was with the Iraqi unit when they were engaged and that on the morning of the 27th, the unit had received small arms fire. He also said that the body of the Iraqi that Sandoval had shot was found very near to the location where the MiTT team had been attacked that morning. The shooting had occurred in an area called the Buhayrat.

It was important for our defense to establish not only that an Iraqi military officer had identified the body as an insurgent but also that this was a very dangerous place. In questions about the safety of the area, Mulvaney provided us a written sworn statement with the exact answers we were looking for. He told us that the area around FOB Iskan was "very dangerous, where avenues of approach were mined with IEDs, and troops were guaranteed to encounter resistance with small arms fire." Additionally, he confirmed that the tactics, techniques, and procedures the insurgents in the area employed were to "engage us with light machine guns or automatic weapons and, upon us advancing, the insurgents will retrograde and attempt to blend into the surroundings, essentially run away."

The information that Mulvaney was providing was extremely helpful to the case, but also frightening considering that McCray and I had just walked down one of these same "very dangerous" roads to get to the MiTT team.

Mulvaney signed his statement, which contained great

information about the insurgents in the area and the shooting of 27 April 2007. His statement was dated 18 August 2007 and later, in phone interviews with both sides, his stipulated testimony was agreed upon. (His stipulated testimony would be read to the military panel at the time of Sandoval's trial because Mulvaney had left Iraq to go home only weeks before the trial; both sides agreed that he did not need to fly back to testify as his version of events was essentially uncontested.) I felt that his statement and stipulated testimony carried immense weight because he was in a completely different unit and command than Sandoval and was actually present for some of the events surrounding 27 April 2007.

◆ ◆ ◆

CAPTAIN DOUGLAS MULVANEY, STIPULATED TRIAL TESTIMONY

It is hereby stipulated by and between the defense and the government, with the express consent of SPC Jorge G. Sandoval, Jr., that the following statement of expected testimony be introduced without objection at trial in the government's or defense's case:

If called to testify, CPT Douglas J. Mulvaney, U.S. Army, of Military Transition Team (MiTT) 0842, Iraqi Assistance Group, FOB Iskan, Iraq, would testify as follows:

CPT Mulvaney was an advisor to the 2/4/8 Iraq Army Division around 27 April 2007. As a member of a MiTT team he lived with and trained the Iraqi Army. Members of MiTT teams often participate in missions and, if necessary, call in U.S. air support and provide direct battle assistance. The 2/4/8 Iraqi Army Division that CPT Mulvaney supported operated in Iskandariyah, Iraq. CPT Mulvaney's job included advising and training the Iraqi Army units in the area on military operations and he went on combat operations with them.

On 27 April 2007 at 0600, CPT Mulvaney was on a combat patrol with the Iraqi Army and scouts from the 1-501st Infantry. The patrol was in the Buhayrat area of Iraq, which is located near FOB Iskan. The Abu Shemsi area is in the Buhayrat area. The patrol was mounted but eventually dismounted and began patrolling north looking for mortars and weapons caches. Around 0650 the Iraqi Army was attacked with small arms fire by two personnel hidden in the reeds. The personnel fled the area moving to the East. CPT Didier was present, directing sniper teams of the 1-501st in the area and he informed his sniper teams in the area via radio that the attackers were fleeing in the direction of their location.

Around 0740, CPT Mulvaney received a report on the radio that the U.S. sniper team had engaged and killed one insurgent matching the same description that was passed to them via radio earlier. CPT Mulvaney did not witness the sniper team engage.

Later that morning, Lieut. Ashraf Sakhi, an Iraqi Army Intelligence Officer, instructed his Iraqi Army soldiers to search the general area where the personnel who attacked them had been located. A weapons cache was uncovered containing mortars, grenades, fuses, and firearms. No command wire was found in the cache.

Later that day, CPT Mulvaney received a call to connect with the snipers and transport the body the rest of the way back to Forward Operating Base Iskandariyah. At the linkup point, CPT Mulvaney took the body to Lieut. Ashraf Sakhi to see if he could identify the remains. The man's head was covered at the time Lieut. Sakhi inspected the body. Lieut. Sakhi identified him as one of the insurgents who had attacked them that morning."

♦ ♦ ♦

LIEUT. ASHRAF SABAH SAKHI, IRAQI ARMY

After signing his statement, Mulvaney told us that he would try to find the Iraqi officer so we could speak with him. A few minutes later, Mulvaney, an Iraqi officer, and an interpreter appeared. Through the interpreter, the officer was introduced as Lieutenant "Ashe." Ashe served as the Iraqi Army's Intelligence Officer for the operational area of Iskan. He was clean shaven with a mustache and appeared to be in his late twenties. He was strikingly more clean-cut than the other Iraqi soldiers in the compound, and it was evident by his uniform and appearance that he was an officer.

Through the interpreter, McCray and I introduced ourselves and explained that we were investigating the death of 27 April and were defending a U.S. soldier who was charged with murdering the person. It was clear that Ashe had been told why we were there, and he quickly informed us that he had been the one to identify the body as an insurgent. We then asked all sorts of questions about that day and the details of the shooting.

Ashe was quick to talk to us but when we asked him to essentially put his money where his mouth was to confirm what he was saying in writing, he began to waffle. Nonetheless, after an hour of persuasion, he agreed to provide a written statement of what happened, as follows: "The Buhayrat area is a very dangerous place; it is controlled by Al Qaeda terrorist groups…The most important terrorist operations are planting improvised explosive devices, kidnapping civilians, attacking the American forces, Iraqi Army, Iraqi Police, and mortar attacks on Iskandariyah…"

When asked, "How can you distinguish between the terrorists' and civilians' clothing?" he replied, "There is a formal opinion from terrorist scholars for everyone to dress in dark colors clothing, especially black. It represents 'Jihad'

Holy War. Also, it is forbidden to shave their beards."

When asked, "What do the civilians wear in this area and how can you distinguish between them and others?" Ashe replied, "It is a farming area, countryside, they dress in typical Arab dress, which is dishdasha and shemagh 'turban.'"

When asked what he was doing on the morning of the 27th, Ashe told us that he had been out on a patrol with the Iraqi Army and U.S. forces when they encountered terrorists sleeping near a canal. As they approached, the terrorists fled. Ashe did not recall specifically that the Iraqi Army received small arms fire; however, he definitely remembered seeing the insurgents and watching them flee. The area where the insurgents were hiding was searched as were the river banks near the terrorists' bedding.

"…We found mortars, grenades, and explosive devices," Ashe continued. "Then we started going back to the FOB when the Americans mentioned that one of the terrorists was shot and killed by an American sniper…. So, we waited until the Americans brought the body. Then I inspected the body, but his face was covered."

When asked about the specifics of how he identified the body as that of an insurgent, Ashe stated that he based his identification on the fact that, "He was not an innocent man. He escaped as soon as he saw us—the American and Iraqi forces—and that was not innocent man behavior. Plus, there are only two families left in that area, and they are all women."

When asked, "Did the deceased's clothing help you in your evaluation of him being a terrorist?" he replied: "For sure, because he was wearing what the terrorists and criminals wear, not like what the farmers wear; besides all farmers at the countryside were sleeping at that time, so what was he doing?"

When asked if he could explain how the deceased could be an insurgent if he did not have a weapon on him, Ashe replied: "If it is an intense fight with the terrorists, they try to escape with their weapon, but if they cannot continue, they throw their weapon in the river or canals or fields so we cannot find it and, as soon as we leave the area, they come back looking for it."

After meeting with Mulvaney and Ashe, we put back on all our body armor, checked our sidearms, and walked back up the road to FOB Iskan. That night we reviewed all the information that we learned and prepared for the continuation of the Article 32 the following morning.

It was time for closing arguments or, as they're called in an Article 32 proceeding, a "comment on the evidence." So that next morning, I attempted to lay out the argument that the shooting was the correct call based on the then-known circumstances. I then argued the additional defense that even if it was not the correct call, the decision to shoot or not shoot was not Sandoval's call to make, and that any fault should be solely with the observer and senior soldier on the ground—Hensley.

I analogized that what Sandoval did by following the sniper manual was no different than when an artilleryman fires a long-range round miles away to an unknown location after receiving a radio call from a forward observer who provides coordinates and asks that an area be destroyed. Additionally, Sandoval's actions were no different than the actions taken by an airman in a missile silo who turns a key to launch an intercontinental ballistic missile after receiving a call on a telephone from someone, somewhere else, to launch.

It has been a common maxim in the military justice field since after the World War II Nazi war crime prosecutions and Nuremburg that "following orders is not a defense." However, that maxim only works where the order is illegal, and the one following it knows it is illegal. In Sandoval's case, even if the order to shoot was illegal, Sandoval would have had no way of knowing it was illegal with his limited visibility of the person as he was laying completely flat against the ground serving in the position of the shooter.

What had become evident at the Article 32 was that Sandoval was being judged for what he did on a field of battle. He was being judged in the 20/20 hindsight of lawyers and investigators, not the 20/400, dirty, scared, and unclear vision of a field of battle. He made the decision to aim, squeeze, and fire his rifle, and I was becoming convinced that he had made the right call—or at a minimum, a call that he was permitted by law to make. The mission of Sandoval's sniper team was to find insurgents emplacing mortar rounds and to kill them. And on the morning of 27 April, that is exactly what Sandoval did.

CPT McCray and I both left FOB Iskan feeling confident that at least the murder charge would go away. I boarded a Blackhawk helicopter for a night flight back to my office at Anaconda, confident that the investigating officer would recommend dismissing the murder charge, and that the entire case might possibly go away with something less than a court-martial.

Optimistically I thought, *the Article 32 Investigating Officer will just recommend some minor punishment or misdemeanor level proceeding for the charge of planting the command wire on the deceased's body.*

SEVEN - THE SHOOTING OF 11 MAY 2007

"A person who aids, abets, counsels, commands, or procures the commission of an offense, or who causes an act to be done which, if done by that person directly, would be an offense is equally guilty of the offense as one who commits it directly, and may be punished to the same extent."

~ ***"Principals," Article 77, Uniform Code of Military Justice***

In the first week of August, I received an email informing me that the investigating officer had recommended that both the 27 April 2007 murder charge and the planting of command wire charges go forward to a general court-martial. I was very upset and frankly dumbfounded. I couldn't imagine what "reasonable grounds" the investigating officer could have found to support the murder charge.

Soon thereafter, I received more shocking news. On 5 August 2007, Sandoval's company commander, Captain (CPT) Charles Levine, signed additional charges against Sandoval.

This second charge sheet added under "Additional Charge I" the charge of murder related to the 11 May 2007 incident, as follows:

Additional Charge I: Violation of the UCMJ, Article 118

Specification:*In that Specialist Jorge G. Sandoval, Jr., U.S. Army did, at or near Jurf as Sakhr, Iraq, on or about 11 May 2007, with premeditation, murder Genei*

Nesir Khudair Al-Janabi by means of shooting him with a 9mm pistol.

Additional Charge II: Violation of the UCMJ, Article 92

Specification 1: In that Specialist Jorge G. Sandoval, Jr., U.S. Army, who knew of his duties, at or near Jurf as Sakhr, Iraq, on or about 11 May 2007, was derelict in the performance of his duties in that he failed to ensure the humane treatment of a detainee, as it was his duty to do.

Specification 2: In that Specialist Jorge G. Sandoval, Jr., U.S. Army, who knew of his duties, at or near Jurf as Sakhr, Iraq, and at or near Forward Operating Base Iskandariyah, Iraq, from between on or about 11 May 2007 and on or about 27 June 2007, was derelict in the performance of those duties in that he willfully failed to report the murder of a detainee, as it was his duty to do.

Additional Charge III: Violation of the UCMJ, Article 134

Specification: In that Jorge G. Sandoval, Jr., U.S. Army, did, at or near Jurf as Sakhr, Iraq, on or about 11 May 2007, wrongfully place an AK-47 rifle with the remains of Genei Nesir Khudair Al-Janabi, which conduct was to the prejudice of the good order and discipline in the armed forces or of a nature to bring discredit upon the armed forces.

Basically, the additional charges consisted of the premeditated murder of a Mr. Genei Nesir Khudair Al-Janabi on 11 May 2007 by means of shooting him with a 9mm pistol, dereliction of duty by providing inhumane treatment to Mr. Al- Janabi, dereliction of duty by not reporting the murder of Mr. Al-Janabi to the chain of command, and wrongfully placing an AK-47 rifle on the body of Mr. Al-Janabi.

As Sandoval recalls, "I was already in pretrial confinement at the time I received notice of a second set of charges related to 11 May. I was eating dinner at the Kuwaiti confinement facility when one of guards came up to me.

"'Hey,' he said. 'I've got some bad news for you. Would you like the news right now or after you finish eating?'

"I looked at him and continued eating. Then I said, 'What the hell—go ahead and tell me right now.'

"When the guard put an additional charge sheet in front of me, I thought to myself, *Oh, wow*... I didn't have time to think and didn't want to think about it. I was only afforded fifteen minutes to eat before I would be sent back to my confinement cell so I sat and finished my horrible meal.

"Either that same night or the following morning, the psychiatric doctor for the facility, a Navy Lieutenant Commander, pulled me to another section of the facility and said, 'One of the guards notified me that you seemed a little distraught. He said you might have cussed a little bit when you received the second set of charges. So I wanted to follow up with you and see how you felt.'

"In so many words, he was trying to find out whether the bad news made me want to hurt myself or anyone else.

"'I'm perfectly fine,' I said. But I thought to myself, *How else would I react to that kind of news? What the hell?!*"

♦ ♦ ♦

Sandoval recalls the specifics of 11 May 2007:

We had been working at the Jurf Al Sakhar control base.[18] We had gone on maybe one or two missions before 11 May 2007. We were all pretty exhausted, doing twenty-four-hour

---

18   The Jurf Al Sakhar control base was a small base located away from FOB Iskan near the town of Jurf Al Sakhar. The base was located South of Baghdad and was a starting point from where the sniper units would come and go for missions.

missions at a time. When we'd get back from a mission, we were so dog tired and yet we still had to debrief and make sure all our equipment was accounted for.

We would have just enough time to get a few hours of sleep before the sun came up. We would be sleeping outside in the open, and by seven or eight o'clock in the morning, it was unbearably hot during that time of year. So, we'd get very little sleep. It would get so hot we would be frying and looking for any piece of shade, anywhere that it was a little cooler. We were always pretty tired.

The night before the 11 May mission, we were moving out in the early morning hours after midnight around two or three o'clock. The sun had set around eight-thirty or nine o'clock at night which is comparable to the summer weather where I'm from in Laredo, Texas. We had gone over the perimeter barriers of the control base because we wanted to avoid being seen leaving out of the front gate.

The enemy was monitoring our movements, and we were being watched at all times. They would time when the convoys and patrols would go out and tell their insurgent friends, "You've got a patrol coming your way!"

So, we'd gone over the perimeter barriers and then we crossed in full equipment with our rucksacks and everything and proceeded into the objective area. The objective that night was to provide overwatch and target interdiction because Alpha Company, I believe, was going to conduct a raid of a certain area there.

Our mission was to interdict targets either coming in or going out. Right after we'd left the base, we were walking single file and before we had walked very far at all, these Iraqi policemen racked their AK-47s, came at us and started saying something. We weren't fluent in Arabic and didn't understand a word they were saying—and it was dark so we couldn't see them. There were no streetlights. All we had to go on was the direction that the sound was coming from.

Hearing the racking of the AK-47s, my heart was pounding so fast, I didn't know what to do. Sergeant Hensley was out in front of the formation that night. It was Sergeant Hensley, then Hand, Redfern, Vela, and me.

Hensley said, in the direction the sound had come from, "Hi" or "Hey" and then he said, "My name is Mike! Don't shoot."

That area was a hotbed for insurgency, and the Iraqi Army was very jumpy. Prior to that incident, we'd already had a couple of green-on-blue incidents. Hensley defused the situation. He said something to them about us being friendly Americans. It was so dark they couldn't see our uniforms and hadn't realized that we were military.

Hensley carefully walked up a little closer to the Iraqi policemen to talk to them. Then he came back and said to us, "Let's move."

We proceeded with our movement, going down people's backyards all the way to the objective. We all separated. He sent Redfern and Hand and Vela to overwatch the area. Me and Hensley hung back a little bit as a sort of fallback position, a command control element for our guys.

Once the rest of the team broke off, Hensley and I sat together for a while. Hensley always packed light for these missions. He might've had an assault pack with MRE and his radio and weapon but he didn't have much. I would always carry a rucksack with a lot of water. Even if I didn't need it someone would end up needing it. A lot of guys try to be hard asses and save themselves a little bit of fatigue by saving their water. I was never one of those. I know that if you're dehydrated, you can't function well.

Any time we came from a mission, Hensley would have to debrief our movements. That would take anywhere from an hour to a few hours and then he'd have to start prepping for the next mission. He never got a lot of sleep and he was always very sleep deprived.

So, when the rest of the guys broke off and left, Hensley said to me, "Hey, do you have a poncho?"

"I've got a wet weather poncho, yeah."

"Can I borrow it?" he asked. "I just want to lay down here for a little bit. Can you monitor the radio?"

Hensley was always concerned with our health as his soldiers. The first thing he would do after a mission was say, "Hey, I'll take care of the debrief. Go get some chow and get some rest." So I could totally understand how he'd be more fatigued than us. I had no problem with it and gave him my poncho.

He lay down and passed out. That was alright with me and perfectly understandable.

I was monitoring the radio when the leadership from Alpha Company radioed us. We were done. We were pulling out. There was no incident.

I woke up Hensley and said, "It's over. What do you want to do?"

"Collapse the team. Call the guys and bring them into our grid. Set up for the rest of the day and see what we see. That's it for the day."

The sun hadn't come up yet for the day when Alpha Company finished the raid. So Hensley instructed me to get the other team collapsed down into our positions so we could pull security. Sergeant Hensley was in charge and he made the decision to drop it down to one-man security and have one guy up at a time.

I don't know why he made that decision. I didn't agree with his decision. There were five of us all within close proximity of each other and I felt that at all times there should be at least two guys.

If I remember correctly, we were doing one-hour sleep shifts. One man would wake up the next man. I think I took the first or second security shift. I had finished my security shift and woke up Vela to do his shift. "Hey, it's your turn," I said and handed him my pistol. "Here you go and here's the radio." The radio was already set on a certain frequency.

We all understood what we had to do. I had said, "Here's the pistol…here's the radio," and then I went to my piece of real estate and passed out. I woke up to what in my mind, being asleep, I could only conceive as grunting noises or something. I woke up to this man standing in front of me, five or six feet away, babbling something in Arabic. I noticed that he was older than us, probably in his late thirties.

My first thought was, *What the fuck?*

I tried to regain my focus. Everyone else was passed out. I looked over to my left because that's where I had placed my weapon, my sniper rifle. While I slept, I had rolled away from my weapon. It was now further than arm's length away. I was taught never to have my weapon further than arm's length. I wanted to put out my hand and grab it but I didn't want to make any sudden moves.

All sorts of thoughts were going through my mind—thoughts like, *I hope this guy doesn't hurt or kill me! I hope he doesn't throw a grenade or have a weapon I haven't seen.*

I was still lying on my back, looking up and I put my chin up. SGT Vela was off to the side of me on top of a little berm. I thought, *Oh, man, this guy's asleep during his shift!*

Because Sergeant Vela had fallen asleep during his shift, this guy had been able to walk into our area. Had Vela been awake, that wouldn't have happened.

"Vela, wake up! Wake up!" I said.

Vela was sleeping sitting down, holding a radio in one hand and a pistol in the other and his head was slumped, chin to chest. Vela started to slowly wake up.

"There's a guy standing in front of us," I said. "There's a guy RIGHT THERE! Point your gun at him...or do something!"

Vela said, "Uh...okay," as he was still trying to wake up. I still couldn't reach my gun and didn't want to move. The other guys started to wake up.

I was finally able to grab my weapon and at that point, I went into my training. The guy became a person who had compromised us—a potential threat to our lives. I told him to get down and had him lay down on the ground so we could search him.

This was all really awkward to me. I didn't like having this responsibility of telling others what to do. I was just a Specialist. There were Sergeants with me, and this was what they should have been doing.

I now had my gun with me and I was pointing it at the guy. I didn't know who he was. If we hadn't woken up, he might have slit our throats. Or maybe he would have told someone he found five Americans sleeping.

At a time like that, your training kicks in. I told Redfern, "Search him! See if he's got anything."

So Redfern searched him and didn't find anything. By that time, Hensley had woken up and took over the situation. He ordered me and Redfern to go and pull security in a pump house in the area. He ordered Hand the other way, over the berm we were at. We went our way and they went their way. Vela stayed with Hensley. After that, the rest was history.

The pump house was a small brick building about six feet by six feet that contained an old gasoline pump that pumped water out of the river into the fields for irrigation.[19] When Sandoval and Redfern arrived at the pump house, they each

---

19   NOTE: A hand-drawn picture by Redfern of the pump house and surrounding area is included in the middle section of the book.

set up their respective sectors of fire[20] focused on ensuring that other Iraqis in the area were not also approaching. Behind Sandoval and Redfern was the pump house wall, and twenty meters behind that wall were Hensley, Vela, and the older man. Hand pulled security from a berm about two meters in the opposite direction of Sandoval and Redfern.

The three dispatched snipers—Hand, Sandoval, and Redfern—pulled security for several minutes when they heard shots fired from where Vela and Hensley were waiting with the Iraqi man. Hensley issued directions for all the snipers to consolidate back to his position. It was at that point that all the snipers clearly saw the Iraqi man dead on the ground. None of them witnessed the actual shooting. Hensley told them he had reported the shooting on the radio. Thereafter, an SSE team arrived, photographed the body, and recorded the shooting. None of the snipers reported the shooting as anything other than a shooting, and no one accused Vela of doing anything wrong. It was later determined that the deceased man was Mr. Al-Janabi.

♦ ♦ ♦

Prior to Sandoval receiving this second charge sheet, I was already familiar with the circumstances surrounding 11 May 2007. The events of that day had been fully investigated during the Article 32 because Hensley had been charged with essentially the same crimes against Mr. Al-Janabi. I had heard all the evidence against Hensley during the original Article 32 and could not understand why Sandoval had been charged with anything at all related to that day.

At the time of the original Article 32, only Hensley and Vela were charged with the murder of Mr. Al-Janabi. The

---

20   A sector of fire is the term for simply looking at terrain like a clock and directing what locations of the terrain each person will monitor with their weapon. For example, "I have your six" would refer to the six-o-clock rear location.

documentary evidence and the testimony at the Article 32 offered little insight into what really happened on 11 May, but one thing was clear: Vela shot an Iraqi local national in the head with a 9mm pistol at close range, killing him instantly. Vela was an experienced combat soldier, but just like Sandoval's kill of 27 April, this was Vela's first and only kill.

Between 24 and 25 June, Vela made three sworn statements to CID. These three statements were obtained during ten hours of interrogation and each contained wildly different versions of how the 11 May shooting occurred. The only consistent portions of Vela's statements were that on the morning of 11 May, he, Hensley, Sandoval and other snipers were on a multiple-day sniper mission. Their mission was similar to Sandoval's 27 April mission. After three days of nearly nonstop reconnaissance and security in the area, the snipers consolidated in a hide-site area to rest for the night and early morning. Vela pulled security on the morning of 11 May while the other snipers slept. At some point, an Iraqi male later identified as Mr. Al-Janabi came into the hide-site, and Vela shot him in the head at close range, twice.

In Vela's first version of events, Hensley and he were awake in the hide-site when Vela saw a man 150 yards from the hide-site armed with a rifle approaching the hide-site. While keeping eyes on the man, Hensley radioed to his superiors requesting permission for a "close kill." A close kill is where an individual is killed in very close proximity to the shooter, and it is generally accomplished with a handgun or knife. A close kill is rare on the battlefield because the closer the enemy is allowed to come towards a soldier, the more dangerous the encounter. Such a killing is only accomplished if operationally necessary, such as when a soldier does not want to give away his location until the last minute, and permission from higher command is generally required.

FIRST SWORN STATEMENT OF
SERGEANT EVAN VELA

According to Vela, Hensley requested permission, and command granted authority for the close kill. Then Hensley grabbed the man, and Vela shot him. It was unclear from Vela's first version of events where the other snipers were in the hide-site or if they participated in the shooting.

According to Vela:

"...Sometime before noon, I spotted an individual roughly 350 to 400 meters southeast of my position. I notified SSG Hensley and was told to maintain eyes on. We identified a weapon on the person when he got about 150 to 175 meters out. SSG Hensley called up on the radio asking permission to do a close kill in an attempt to keep our position from being compromised. We were going to use the pistol as opposed to a rifle. SSG Hensley said that he was going to grab him to keep him under control and I grabbed the pistol. At this time, we had still not notified the sniper team in the pump house.

When the person moved to about 5 to 6 degrees north of our position, SSG Hensley grabbed the guy, pulled him close to him with the guy's back to SSG Hensley's front and turned slightly south. I then delivered two shots with my 9mm pistol to the individual's head, one to the left side of the guy's head while SSG Hensley grabbed him, and the other once he had hit the ground to the forehead of the guy. About 5 or 10 minutes later, SSE then came to take pictures and collect up the body…

◆ ◆ ◆

STAFF SERGEANT MICHAEL ANTHONY HENSLEY

Hensley had given a sworn statement to CID on 24 June in response to questions about the deaths of six Iraqis on three separate missions. Hensley's statement about the 11 May shooting was similar to Vela's in the sense that the Iraqi walked up on them in the hide-site armed, and they felt the man was a threat and would give away their position. Hensley's statement also echoed Vela's in that he admitted to having grabbed the man and placed him in a chokehold while Vela shot him.

According to Hensley:

...The possible enemy was moving very slowly and cautiously toward my position, obviously probing for something. I did not engage or show myself because this guy I wanted to detain. At approximately 100 meters out, I noticed by the facial expression on the guy's face that he had made a member of my heavy team.[21] After that he stayed hidden for about five minutes and then he felt safe enough to move toward my heavy team position. What he didn't see was that myself and SGT Vela were behind a berm in between him and his target which, by the way, was one of my soldiers.

I wanted to detain him as he passed by my position and toward the pump house. I told SGT Vela to prep the pistol in the event that we needed to conduct a close kill. As the local national passed by my position, unaware of mine or SGT Vela's existence, he was still fixated on my soldiers with God knows what intent. I then assumed a position behind him and placed him in a rear naked choke.[22] He was still struggling

---

21   By this representation of being "made" it is believed that Hensley was implying that their location had been compromised.

22   A rear naked choke is a chokehold used in martial arts and applied from an opponent's back.

with his weapon so I had SGT Vela shoot him in the head. He placed two rounds into the head of the local national.

I felt that trying to detain the local national was not worth losing a soldier's life over. The decision to shoot this armed insurgent was based on a reaction to a lethal threat that he was placing within 15 meters of my snipers and, in my mind, this was the only way to place an end to the threat...

Hensley had provided a similar sworn statement to his battalion leadership later in the day on 11 May when there was an informal inquiry as to how the man died. It was alleged by the prosecutors at the first Article 32 that Hensley had shown his original statement to Vela, Redfern, Hand, and Sandoval after he wrote it, urging them to read it and to stick with that version of events if ever questioned.

It was also alleged by the prosecutors that Hensley fabricated that version of events and then attempted to influence the other snipers. That allegation was not substantiated at the first Article 32 as no one testified that they recalled reading it and being asked to stick with that version. Rather Hand and Redfern testified that they were shown the statement because everyone was spread out that morning and no one truly knew what had occurred. They testified that it did not influence what they told the command and CID about what happened on 11 May.

◆ ◆ ◆

SECOND SWORN STATEMENT OF SERGEANT EVAN VELA

There were contradictions and inconsistencies from one Vela statement to the next and within the statements themselves. Vela's second version of events told an entirely different story than his first.

According to Vela's second version, at some point an unknown Iraqi male walked into the location where the snipers were resting. No one saw him coming, and his presence startled them. They detained the man and bound his hands together as they were trying to find out who he was and why he was there. The man did not speak English, and while the snipers were trying to communicate with him, a young Iraqi boy approached, seemingly looking for the man. The snipers also detained the boy. The man began yelling and talking loudly and the snipers attempted to quiet him by placing clothing over the man's head.

According to Vela:

The next morning, SPC Sandoval and I were awake on our guard. A local national walked into our position, and I did not see him due to my position. I looked at Sandoval, and it looked like he had been motioning to me to let me know that someone was walking up on our hide. I picked the pistol up and began pulling security on the local national. Once Sandoval had eyes on him, I woke up SGT Hand and let him know that someone had walked into our hide and to pull security towards the [illegible] area. SGT Redfern was woken up and then began to search the local national and found nothing on him. The individual was placed face down on the ground and I woke SSG Hensley...

At some point, according to this second statement, all the other snipers present were placed on perimeter security position, and just Vela and Hensley remained in the middle of the hide-site. A few minutes later, Hensley radioed for permission for a close kill. Command authorized the close kill.

Vela continued:

...I motioned to the person, and we upped our security by placing Redfern and SPC Sandoval in the pump house to our northeast. About a half an hour later, a boy walked into our hide. Prior to that, SSG Hensley asked if we searched, we said yes, so he then went up to the person, put his knee on his back and told him to be quiet and tied his hands. He said this because the person was sobbing and crying. We then moved him to the berm and let him position himself. After detaining the boy, SSG Hensley finally said, "I will let the boy go but this guy is not going anywhere." I was not completely clear on his intent.

He then called up to higher and said, "We have a guy 400 meters out with an AK-47." The call came back with, "If you have PID, you are clear to engage." SSG Hensley said, "We will continue to monitor him to see if he comes closer." He then asked permission to do a close kill, and I did not hear the response. He then however untied the person's hands and put his head dress over his head and tilted his head. He then looked at me, said, "Are you ready," said "Shoot," and jumped out of the way. I shot as told by SSG Hensley at the person's head.

SSG Hensley then placed the AK on the person. The person was still moving and so SSG Hensley then said, "Shoot him again." SSG Hensley said, "If anyone asks, here's what happened. I grabbed the guy and Vela shot him. You three [SGT Hand, SGT Redfern and SPC Sandoval] did not see anything because you were in the pump house."

Vela never said that Sandoval was present in the middle of the hide-site at the time of the kill nor did he implicate him in planting the AK-47. The only thing Vela mentioned in any of his statements about Sandoval was in his first statement when asked, "What was Sandoval's reaction to the killing of the local national?"

Vela responded, "He kind of congratulated me. He looked at me and gave me a head nod." There were no follow-up questions about when exactly the head nod took place or what it meant.

In Vela's second statement, he specifically said that "SPC Sandoval did not see anything because they were in the pump house." This was again confirmed in the section of Vela's third and final statement where he was asked about the location of Sandoval during the shooting and he answered, "in the pump house."

When Sandoval was questioned by CID, he was never asked about the 11 May shooting because at that time, the CID Special Agent interrogating Sandoval did not have evidence that he had anything to do with the shooting. Thus, the only written versions of what happened were the sworn statements of Vela, Hensley, and the other snipers.

These statements of Vela's differ from Sandoval's recollection of events. For one thing, Vela states that he and Sandoval were "awake on our guard" whereas Sandoval states that after pulling security, he was on his sleep shift and awoke to find the Iraqi National standing in their hide-site and Vela *asleep* on his security shift.

Vela never mentioned being asleep on his security shift. Falling asleep while on guard duty is an extremely serious offense as it endangers the entire unit who are sleeping and trusting that the guard is doing his job. However, it is worth noting that Vela makes it a point in his first statement to say, "From the way I was oriented, I did not see the local national walk into the hide…" As such, he is admitting at least to some extent that he was not doing a very good job of being on guard duty.

If you'll recall, Sandoval remembers the situation this way: "I was still lying on my back, looking up, and I put my chin up. SGT Vela was off to the side of me on top of a little berm. I thought, *Oh, man, this guy's asleep during his shift!*

"'Vela, wake up! Wake up!' I said.

"Vela was sleeping sitting down, holding a radio in one hand and a pistol in the other and his head was slumped, chin to chest. Vela started to slowly wake up.

"'There's a guy standing in front of us,' I said. 'There's a guy RIGHT THERE! Point your gun at him…or do something!'

"Vela said, 'Uh…okay' as he was still trying to wake up."

Under the UCMJ, when someone knowingly and willingly counsels, commands, or procures another to commit an offense, that person is also a principal and is therefore just as guilty as the person who personally committed the offense. However, mere presence at the scene of a crime or simply failing to prevent a crime is not enough to convict on a principal theory. There must be intent to aid or encourage someone to commit the crime. In this instance, there was zero evidence of any intent to aid or encourage on the part of Sandoval, and as such he was not acting as a "principal" and not guilty of the murder.

I believed that at most, the facts showed that perhaps Sandoval should have questioned Vela and Hensley about what had happened to the Iraqi man. However, I did not believe for one second that the fact that Sandoval chose not to question his superior non-commissioned officers equated to murder or complacency to murder.

These new charges against Sandoval related to 11 May had not been considered by the investigating officer at the original Article 32. Therefore, the Article 32 was re-opened to investigate the additional charges and was set to occur in the courtroom at the Victory Base Complex, the massive U.S. compound just outside of Baghdad that surrounds the Baghdad International Airport.

EIGHT – ANOTHER ARTICLE 32 INVESTIGATION

Unlawful command influence (UCI) is any action taken in an attempt to influence either an outcome or another into an inappropriate action regarding the military justice process. UCI may occur in attempts to influence court members, witnesses, or commanders in whether or not to charge or punish soldiers for misconduct as it undermines the independent discretion of the military command to decide each event on a case-by-case basis. The United States Court of Military Appeals has defined UCI as the "mortal enemy of military justice."

~ United States v. Thomas, 22 M.J. 388, 393 (Court of Military Appeals 1986)

By this point in time, my former co-counsel, Captain McCray, had completed her tour in Iraq and gone on to her next assignment in Washington, D.C. As a result, Captain (CPT) Erik Claudio from the Anaconda Trial Defense office was detailed to serve as co-counsel. Given the severity of the charges and the almost complete certainty that the case would proceed to trial rather than conclude in a plea bargain, the leadership of the U.S. Army Trial Defense Service wanted to make sure that I had an experienced co-counsel to assist with both the investigation of the case and at trial.

Claudio was a very experienced former prosecutor who had recently deployed to Iraq after serving as a Trial Defense Counsel in Germany. He had a significant amount of trial experience and I was glad to have him join the team. As the case progressed, Claudio was able to provide welcome feedback related to trial strategy, the examination of witnesses, and the defense theory of the case. Sandoval also liked Claudio. This all played well into building the best defense team that we could to take on the extremely serious charges.

Claudio and I arrived at the Victory Base Complex adjacent to Baghdad on the evening of 16 August, hitchhiking our way via military buses to the U.S. Army Trial Defense Headquarters for Iraq, Afghanistan, and Kuwait. The headquarters was located in a former mansion in the Victory Complex that overlooked the Tigris River. That night, Claudio and I reviewed the file again and role-played testimony. In the early morning hours, we fell asleep on cots in rooms that doubled as offices and sleeping quarters. We were exhausted from the travel and game-planning, but we were confident that we were also prepared.

After catching a little shut-eye, we awoke and hitched a ride a few miles away to what is known as Camp Liberty— one of the camps situated on the Victory Base Complex compound, along with Camp Striker and Camp Slayer. In the early days of the U.S. invasion, each camp served as its own base and was situated at different locations around the Baghdad International Airport (formerly the Saddam International Airport) separated by walls and checkpoints. However, as the U.S. forces remained in place, roads with high walls were built, combining all the compounds into one. Although the separated areas then comprised one complex named Victory, the separate locations in the complex still retained their individual names.

Camp Liberty was located in the northernmost area of the complex and had its own courthouse located at the bottom of Tower Hill, so named because it was the highest point in the camp and had numerous communication towers erected there. The hill was the constant target of Iraqi insurgents who liked to fire mortars at the hill because they could see the towers from outside of camp and it provided a good targeting point.

Prior to the first day of the re-opened Article 32, I sent a letter to Sandoval's Brigade Commander formally objecting to the re-appointment of Major Hasse as the investigating officer. Such action by the prosecution and command reeked of unlawful command influence.

My objection to reopening the Article 32 investigation was based on the fact that it was occurring after the original Article 32 investigation had closed. After the original Article 32, Sandoval's Brigade Commander had recommended that the original charges be sent to a general court-martial, and the Commanding General of the 3rd Infantry Division followed that recommendation. The new set of charges being investigated were preferred in the interim; however, they could have been preferred earlier if Hasse had recommended that Sandoval also be charged with the 11 May shooting.

The events of 11 May had already been investigated as part of the original Article 32 as they related to SSG Hensley. Major Hasse had ample opportunity to review all the evidence and make any determinations whether Sandoval had committed a crime on 11 May and recommend new charges if he had felt they were appropriate. Under Rule for Court-Martial 405(e), "If evidence during the investigation indicates that the accused committed an uncharged offense, the investigating officer may investigate the subject matter of such offense and make a recommendation as to its disposition without the accused first having been charged with the offense."

Hasse had not made any such recommendation for additional charges. Because of this, for the Brigade Commander to now direct that the same investigating officer investigate the same facts, without providing any new substantial evidence, was the equivalent of saying, "I don't like your first findings. Look again."

Following is an excerpt of my letter:

"...It is obvious that MAJ Hasse did not find that the evidence indicated that the accused committed any additional uncharged offenses as he did not list any. To now force new charges on MAJ Hasse with no new substantial evidence after the Commanding General has referred the original charges to court-martial is to in effect say, 'I do not think your first findings are complete; go back and re-examine the same evidence and find that these new charges should go forward to court-martial as well.'

There is an omnipresent threat of actual and perceived influence from you to MAJ Hasse if you ask him to review new charges without new evidence now that the original charges have been referred. Additionally, there is an omnipresent threat of actual and perceived influence from the Commanding General convening authority to you and then down to MAJ Hasse if you ask MAJ Hasse to review new charges without new evidence now that the Commanding General has approved that 'the allegations in the specifications are warranted by the evidence in the report of investigation' and referred such charges and specifications to a general court-martial."

This situation was complete bullshit. The Brigade Commander was essentially asking Hasse to rubber stamp new charges against Sandoval for the 11 May incident. This action clearly showed that the government was not truly requesting that an investigation of the new charges occur, but rather requesting that the charges be deemed "having been investigated." This action was improper and revealed that while the government may have been following formal court-martial procedure, it was clear that they were not interested in an actual, impartial investigation of the charges. Rather, the government needed to claim that the charges had been "investigated" and now that this was completed, they simply wanted their court-martial.

The unlawful command influence was not the strongest

objection as there was no caselaw directly on point. However, out of an abundance of caution, I hoped the Brigade Commander would appoint a new investigating officer. An accused has a right to an impartial Article 32 investigating officer and on appeal, military appellate courts have overturned complete convictions because the Article 32 itself was defective in some form.

I wanted a *new* investigating officer, someone truly independent who would scrutinize the government's estranged theory of culpability and loudly demand dismissal. I was nearly certain that because of the command influence, the current Investigating Officer would simply recommend that all new charges go forward to a general court-martial.

The Brigade Commander denied our objection, and on 17 August 2007, at 0856 in the morning, the re-opened Article 32 was formally called to order. When the re-opened Article 32 began, it took on an ominous tone: no longer was there the hope that the charges would be dismissed or that the investigating officer would make a strong rebuttal to the government's allegations.

As the Article 32 began, we made numerous objections regarding discovery with the government. We had earlier made formal requests for maps, pictures, and intelligence summaries regarding the area of the 11 May shooting as well as training records, briefings, reports, and guidance put out by Sandoval's command regarding the Rules of Engagement and targeting the enemy.

At this point,, none of the requested additional evidence had been provided. I was beginning to get the impression that the government was trying to railroad my client. If they wanted to get me motivated, they had just succeeded. I was more fired up than ever to fight for Sandoval and at this point my inner "Honey Badger"[23] had begun to come to light. I was extremely pissed-off, and it took all my strength to remain cool, calm, and collected.

We had also put in a formal request to Sandoval's Brigade Commander for a team of armed combat soldiers to escort me via helicopter to the location of the 27 April shooting to "look at the locations in relation to SPC Sandoval's mission, the known or perceived enemy in the area, the terrain and locations of the shooter and deceased, the time of day and month, and any known civilians in the area."

This request was denied because, "The area you are requesting to visit is in a very volatile region that is not frequented by Coalition Forces…and would place soldiers at high risk due to the substantial IED and small arms fire threat in the area."[24]

This statement was a good description of the area where the 27 April shooting occurred—extremely dangerous.

Most of our requests, including the crime scene visit, had been denied by the prosecutors, but there was not much that could be done at that point. The Article 32 began over our objections. The positive result of vetting the objections early was that the issues were clearly addressed on the record. That meant that there was now a transcript of the specific requests and the government's specific denials so that they could later be addressed with the military judge, who could in turn order the government to provide the evidence, or access to the crime scene.

As its first witness, the government called Sandoval's company commander, CPT Didier. He had testified at length

---

23   Honey Badger was made popular by a YouTube video showing the badger interacting with larger animals. Essentially, when provoked and needing to fight an enemy much larger or stronger than himself: "Honey Badger just don't care!"

24   NOTE: A copy of the formal denial memorandum is located in the middle of this book.

at the original Article 32 and was being called again by the government, this time to testify about the inhumane treatment charge. He testified as follows:

> (Q: PROSECUTOR)
>
> (A: CPT DIDIER)
>
> Q: Captain Didier, when it comes to detainees, do you have a duty to provide humane treatment to those detainees?
>
> A: Yes.
>
> Q: How do you know that you have that duty?
>
> A: It's part of our ROE.[25] Once we detain them, they get the same treatment as a soldier...

The Rules of Engagement (ROE) are briefed in a general format for all service members annually, applied to specific wars and battlefields by the commanders on the ground, and communicated to the soldiers on the ground by their immediate commander. For example, the ROE may set standards for an area in Iraq that are different than for Afghanistan, and ROE may differ even between areas in Iraq based on how the enemy is acting in a certain area at a given time. During 2007, the ROE was different for each area in Iraq, and varied depending upon the unit operating

---

25   ROE is the acronym for Rules of Engagement—the standards governing the force that may be used against the enemy on the field of battle. The ROE outlines who exactly the enemy is and what steps can be taken in response to killing or capturing the enemy. The inhumane treatment portion of the ROE relates to the way the U.S. has agreed to treat detainees and enemy combatants by being a signatory to the Geneva Conventions and its Protocols. The ROE have their origins in standards developed over centuries about "just warfare" and apply the Geneva Conventions to the battlefield.

in a specific area.[26] The government's examination of Didier continued as follows:

> Q: And do you know when you were briefed on your duty to detainees?
>
> A: Prior to every mission, ma'am. It's part of the ROE brief that's in the patrol book.[27] And again in Kuwait before we got here. That was the whole ROE.
>
> Q: And part of that humane treatment is not abusing detainees, is that correct?
>
> A: Yes.
>
> Q: Part of that humane treatment is also not murdering those detainees, is that correct?
>
> A: Yes.
>
> Q: Specialist Sandoval used to be in your platoon, correct?
>
> A: Yes.
>
> Q: And as part of your platoon he received this kind of briefing?
>
> A: Yes...

The government then questioned Didier about the charge of dereliction of duty by not reporting the murder of 11 May 2007 as follows:

> Q: Captain Didier, when your soldiers see misconduct in the field, are they supposed to report that misconduct

---

26   The generic ROE for U.S. military forces is public information; however, the ROE for a specific mission or area in a combat zone is normally classified information.

27   A patrol is where a small group of soldiers go out on a mission to achieve a specific objective and then return to their home base. A "patrol book" is the written guidance for the unit's particular mission, and outlines all the important details of the mission.

by their soldiers?

A: Yeah.

Q: How do they know that they are supposed to report it?

A: It's part of the Code of Conduct

The Code of Conduct was established by President Dwight D. Eisenhower in 1955 after the Korean War to provide an ethical guide as to how members of the U.S. military should act in combat. Most notably, it gives guidance as to how to act when captured. Article VI of the Code states that, "A member of the armed forces remains responsible for personal actions at all times." I can only guess that this was the portion that the government was referring to during its questioning of CPT Didier. However, based on both the questions and the answers, it was unclear how the Code of Conduct actually played into the prosecution of Sandoval.

The examination of Didier by the government continued, as follows:

Q: And how often are they briefed on the Code of Conduct?

A: We don't brief it—it is part of the seven Army values. I always tell my soldiers that if it's immoral, unethical, or illegal, they have a duty to stop it.

Q: And how often do you go over that with them?

A: I don't know—maybe once in a while.

Q: Once in a while?

A: Yes.

Q: Who are they supposed to report that misconduct to? Do they know?

A: Their chain of command.

Q: And that would be you?

A: Yes.

Q: Are they supposed to report that misconduct immediately as they see it? Or is there a timeline?

A: I would assume immediately if they see it. But I'm sure there are circumstances that can sometimes prevent that. I don't know what those would be, but...

My cross-examination of Captain Didier on his testimony regarding the Code of Conduct went as follows:

Q: Now you talked about misconduct and the reporting of misconduct, and if I am understanding, you said, the Code of Conduct requires that?

A: I believe so, yes. I mean, it's human decency. If you see someone being mistreated that you report that to your chain of command. We all watch the Armed Forces Network commercial that's on constantly talking about it.

Q: Is that the Code of Conduct?

A: I believe so.

As stated above, the Code of Conduct has to do with a soldier himself being captured and does not specifically state anything to do with reporting misconduct. It was my understanding that the government was using the wrong term for what they were implying. Rather, it is the UCMJ that requires a soldier to not conceal misconduct. Concealing a serious offense by not reporting it is considered "Misprision of a Serious Offense" and can be charged under Article 134 of the UCMJ.

I was not trying to belittle CPT Didier but rather to clarify and confirm that he, and apparently the prosecutors, were confused as to what labels they were giving Sandoval's apparent duty to report the shooting. If Didier testified similarly at trial, I planned for him to read the Code of Conduct on the stand and have him attempt to point out to me exactly where it stated that Sandoval had such a duty to report misconduct.

My examination of Didier continued, as follows:

Q: Is it inhumane to detain someone who walks up on your hide-site?

A: No.

Q: Is it inhumane to try to silence them if they are compromising your hide-site?

A: Not as long as you do it without more damage than necessary. As long as you're not beating a person, you can keep them silent as long as you are detaining them and giving them some sort of gag.

Q: But you would agree with me that in some situations you have to take more aggressive action than in others to silence people, correct?

A: Yes.

Q: And then in certain situations it's very important, not only to your safety, but the safety of others, that somebody is in fact silenced, is that correct?

A: Yes.

Q: How many classes did Specialist Sandoval's section receive on dealing with detainees?

A: Specifically his section?

Q: Yes.

A: None as in formally taught classes, but we discussed what happens if someone goes into the hide-site.

Q: What was the nature of the discussion?

A: Usually we would hold them, or they would call it

up and ask us to get higher depending on the scenario of what was taking place.

Q: Now if someone comes up in the hide-site, and they are held in the hide-site, is it then normal that others would then pull security on the outside of the hide-site and make sure others aren't coming up on it?

A: Yes.

Q: And that would actually be the right thing to do, correct?

A: Yes.

Q: And if something were to happen to the person who was detained, then it would be the people who were actually right there on the detainee that were responsible for that, correct?

A: As long as the person who was pulling security didn't know what was going on, yes.

Q: So if they're out pulling security, then their job would be to look outwards, correct?

A: Yes.

Q: And to have a sector of fire, correct?

A: Yes.

Q: And if they're out there doing that and they are focused on that, then they shouldn't be responsible for something that is going on in the middle of the hide-site, should they?

A: No.

Q: And you said that somebody is supposed to report serious incidents to their chain of command, correct?

A: Yes.

Q: Now, a section leader would be in the chain of command, isn't he?

A: Yes.

Q: And do you expect your soldiers to report things even if they don't think they were wrong?

A: If they don't know or don't think something is wrong, then I guess they wouldn't report it because they wouldn't know to.

Q: And this death of 11 May—that was reported to you, wasn't it?

A: Yes.

Q: And, in fact, you authorized it on the radio, correct?

A: Yes.

Q: And you've never seen Specialist Sandoval with an AK-47, have you?

A: No.

After the close of my questioning, the investigating officer asked a few questions, as follows:

Q: Captain Didier, had Specialist Sandoval, or a team, or squad that Specialist Sandoval has been involved with ever detained somebody before?

A: We've held people, but not really detained them. They were civilians and we asked them to stay with us and they did.

Q: But—but when they're in your control, they are your responsibility, so you would consider that a detainee, correct?

A: Yes, sir.

Q: Had you ever had any issues with Specialist Sandoval's conduct with any of the personnel that you had detained up to that point?

A: No, sir.

Q: Had—so the platoon had never had any detainee incidents or issues before?

A: No, sir. And before it was us usually just going into a house that was empty at the time and people would either come home and find us there and we'd ask them to stay, or they were home and we needed to use their home and we'd ask them if we could come in and they would let us.

Q: So you never had any high-value targets or anyone that you had to detain and then process, correct?

A: No.

Q: Do you know of any other incidents within the battalion of detainee abuse? Or heard of any of those at the battalion level?

A: No...

Through its questioning, the government tried to place Sandoval near the shooting in the hide-site as opposed to the perimeter pulling security where most of the statements placed him during the shooting. The government attempted to elicit the incriminating testimony from Captain Didier as follows:

Q: On 11 May, while Staff Sergeant Hensley and his squad were in the field, were you on the radio with Staff Sergeant Hensley?

A: Yes.

Q: From what you heard, did it sound like they were in two different groups?

A: It sounded that way. Well, originally it sounded as though Specialist Sandoval was with him. When he gave me a more detailed report of where guys were, he said that Sergeant Vela and Staff Sergeant Hensley were in one location, and Sergeant Hand, Sergeant Redfern, and Specialist Sandoval were in another one.

Q: And that was when he reported it to you?

A: Yes.

Q: But when you were on the radio with him, did you originally think that perhaps Specialist Sandoval was in the hide-site?

A: For some reason yes, I did.

Q: You did. Thank you very much, Captain Didier.

I was not sure why the government thought it was a good idea to elicit testimony regarding the radio communications between Didier and Hensley as it was not incriminating but rather favorable to the defense. Didier had authorized this shooting on 11 May as well as the 27 April shooting. This was clear as I reminded Didier of his testimony from the original Article 32 in response to questions from Hensley's defense counsel, as follows:

Q: Now, regarding the 11 May 2007 kill, do you recall your testimony at the Article 32 investigation previously?

A: Yes. In reference to what though?

Q: Do you recall giving any testimony?

A: Yes?

Q: Now, regarding some of that questioning regarding the radio communication that you had between you and Staff Sergeant Hensley regarding that kill, do you recall that exchange?

A: Between myself and Staff Sergeant Hensley?

Q: Yes. Do you recall being asked if Staff Sergeant Hensley asked for permission on the close kill?

A: Yes.

Q: And you gave permission, correct?

A: Yes.

Q: And you, in fact, supported that kill, correct?

A: Yes.

Q: And that was the right thing to do. That was the right call, correct?

A: Yes. If it happened the way it was reported to me, then yes.

Q: And if I'm understanding what you just told the Trial Counsel, Staff Sergeant Hensley in fact said that it was only him and Sergeant Vela right next to this person. And Specialist Sandoval was actually in a different building with other people, correct?

A: Not in a different building, but not at that location, yes.

Q: So he was at a completely different location?

A: He was 15 meters away, in what we call another hide-site.

Q: And Staff Sergeant Hensley told you that?

A: Yes. And it is on the follow up report.

In an attempt to minimize this testimony, the government asked the following questions on redirect examination:

Q: Captain Didier, you said in response to both my question and/or both the—Captain Drummond I think asked this twice, that you authorized Staff Sergeant Hensley's kill on 11 May?

A: Yes.

Q: Okay. And that was described to you over the radio?

A: Yes.

Q: What did he say to you over the radio? How did he describe the situation? Can you run through it for the investigating officer? What you heard from Staff Sergeant Hensley over the radio?

A: There was an individual who left an objective another unit had hit the night before and that individual had an AK-47 and he was moving toward their location. He was approximately 100 to 200 meters away and was slowly probing by looking into places where U.S. forces had been. Looking for what we assumed to be stay-behinds, which are what their element was, they were left there to look after the area and to see if something like this happened. I told him to continue watching; hopefully he would lead us to the cache that we were looking for. After about an hour, he said that he was continuing to move slowly and had seen the other element which was 15 meters away from him and was maneuvering on them with the AK-47 and he was going to come right into their hide-site. He asked, if necessary, if he could conduct a close kill. I told him that as the ground forces commander I would authorize that if it was necessary. And about five minutes later, he told me that he had indeed killed the individual. When he came back in, we talked about it. He tried to detain him by taking him down using combatives, but the individual kept his AK-47 pointed at the location where the other hide-site was so he had Sergeant Vela shoot and kill him.

Q: Captain Didier, is it humane to murder a detainee?

A: No.

NINE – THE LOCATION OF THE PUMP HOUSE

"No person subject to this chapter may compel any person to incriminate himself or to answer any questions the answer to which may tend to incriminate him..."

Article 31(a), Uniform Code of Military Justice

The government called Sergeant Robert Redfern as its next witness. He was presumably being called to clarify exactly where everyone was positioned in the hide-site. As the government questioned Redfern, it became immediately apparent that he did not want to be testifying against Sandoval. I was intrigued by the fact that even though Redfern and Hand were also on the 11 May sniper mission and present near the shooting, neither was charged with the 11 May shooting or any crimes related to the shooting. Given the rationale for why Sandoval was charged for 11 May, then both Redfern and Hand should probably have been charged as well, if the government was going to be consistent in its charging theory.

Before being allowed to testify, the government informed Redfern of his rights under Article 31 of the UCMJ. Article 31 rights are similar to the common *Miranda* rights read by police officers to suspects: "You have the right to remain silent; anything you say or do can be held against you in a court of law," etc. Article 31, however, predates the United States Supreme Court's requirements as outlined in the famous *Miranda v. Arizona*[28] case, and places upon the military greater protections for a suspect. Primarily, if a

---

28   *Miranda v. Arizona*, 384 U.S. 436 (1966) is the landmark case that holds that a defendant who is in custody must be notified of their right to an attorney before police questioning.

military member acting in a law enforcement or command role believes that a service member may have committed a crime, then before that service member can be questioned about the crime, that person must be informed of what crime he or she is thought to have committed and his or her rights to counsel.

The fact that Redfern was read his rights told me that the government thought he might have committed a crime, so why didn't the prosecutors charge him—or Hand—with the same crimes as Sandoval? I found this both baffling and frustrating. Just as with other aspects of this case, I was unable to reconcile the government's actions and was left puzzling over why Sandoval—who was simply in the vicinity at the time that Al-Janabi was killed—was charged with his murder while the other individuals like Redfern and Hand—who were also merely in the vicinity—were not charged.

◆ ◆ ◆

SERGEANT ROBERT REDFERN

SGT Redfern's testimony began by the prosecutor asking questions to establish his identity, reading Redfern his Article 31 rights, and confirming that he was volitionally electing to continue with his testimony. Redfern was also informed of the exact charges about which he would be testifying: Murder, under Article 118; Dereliction of Duty, under Article 92; and then Conduct Prejudicial under Article 134.

With these formalities out of the way, the prosecutor then proceeded as follows:

(Q: PROSECUTOR)

(A: SGT REDFERN)

Q: Sergeant Redfern, you were with Specialist

Sandoval, Staff Sergeant Hensley, and Sergeant Vela on 11 May, is that correct?

A: Roger.

Q: And you testified somewhat about the chain of events at the previous Article 32 investigation, is that correct?

A: Roger.

Q: You testified at some point in that Article 32 investigation that at some point while you were in the hide-site with the entire group, you went to a pump house?

A: Yes.

Q: Can you just describe to me what that pump house looked like?

A: Wall behind me. [Redfern gestured with his right arm behind him in a sweeping motion.] Wall beside with a door. [Redfern gestured with his left arm off to his left side.]

Q: Were there any windows in the pump house?

A: No.

Q: Do you remember which direction, if the door is to your left and you're facing and there's a wall to your front. [Prosecutor made a chopping motion with her right hand.] And you're facing the door to your left, which direction is the hide-site?

A: Directly behind me...

Some questions and answers followed related to Redfern's recollection of the exact size of the pump house. Then the prosecutor continued as follows:

Q: When you were in the pump house, Specialist

Sandoval was with you, is that correct?

A: Yes.

Q: Is that true? Okay. That's what you testified before.

A: Yes.

Q: Were the two of you able to both lay in the prone position inside the pump house or were you standing? Sitting?

A: I couldn't tell you.

Q: You said you took turns sleeping, is that correct?

A: Yeah.

Q: Okay, while you were sleeping, were you able to stretch out completely straight inside the pump house?

[Redfern shrugged noncommittally.]

Q: You don't remember?

A: No.

Q: Can you remember if there was a lot of extra space besides the space that you took up and the space that Sandoval took up?

A: Maybe.

Q: How much space?

A: I don't know, maybe a few feet.

Q: You testified at the previous Article 32 investigation that you didn't bring much of your gear with you into the pump house?

A: Roger.

Q: Did you have anything besides yourselves and your weapons?

A: Kit.

Q: Kit? Anything else?

A: Not that I remember.

Q: Where was the river in relation to the pump house?

A: To my right.

Q: Was the pump house directly parallel to the river? The length of the pump house?

A: Maybe.

Q: Was it diagonal?

A: I don't know, it was to my right.

Q: The river was to your right, okay. Was there a pump inside the pump house?

A: Maybe.

More questions followed related to the size of the pump house and how Redfern and Sandoval fit inside. The prosecutor continued as follows:

Q: You said that you heard shots. You popped out. You popped your head out? Describe how you popped your head out.

A: I stuck my head out, looked around. Saw if there was anyone else out there, anyone was coming, and to see where the shots came from.

Q: So when you popped your head out, did you have to scoot over toward the door in order to pop your head out of the door?

A: Yeah.

Q: Scoot over. And do you remember how far you had to scoot?

A: I don't remember.

Q: And do you remember how far away the pump house is from the hide-site? Can you give me an estimate?

A: Between 20 to 30 meters, maybe.

Q: Why were you sent to the pump house?

A: To overwatch the side where no one could see.

Q: If the only opening is the door and you're not looking out that door originally, you said you had to scoot over, how could you overwatch anything inside the pump house?

A: The wall was missing.

Q: Where was the wall missing?

A: About right here. [Redfern gestured with his right arm from the 12 o'clock to the 3 o'clock position.] To the—as I'm looking, the 12 o'clock. [Redfern marked 12 o'clock with his hand.] 3 o'clock. [Redfern marked 3 o'clock with his hand.]

Q: Where was Sandoval inside of the pump house?

A: About a foot away from me...

Several questions followed as to how exactly Redfern and Sandoval were positioned inside the pump house related to each other and the edifice itself and which way they both were facing. Then the prosecutor continued questioning Redfern as follows:

Q: How were you oriented in the pump house? As far as how was your body positioned? Were you both watching the 3 o'clock? Where was he? Where were you facing?

A: He was facing out this way and I was facing out like that. [Redfern demonstrated a classic crossed fields of fire example with his hands.]

Q: Toward the opening? You were facing toward the opening?

A: Yeah, okay—this entire wall is gone. [Redfern gestured to the wall that would be to his right.]

Q: Yes.

A: This wall is a cut out, like half of the wall is missing. [Redfern gestured at the wall that would be ahead of him.]

Q: Half the front wall?

A: Straight ahead.

Q: So you were watching out the front wall and he was watching out the right wall?

A: Yeah. My right, not his right.

Q: And again, that door is to your left?

[Redfern indicated an affirmative response.]

The testimony was beginning to be reminiscent of the famous Abbott and Costello "Who's on first?" comedy routine…[29]

Just as in the Abbott and Costello sketch, everyone in the room was very confused by this point. The questioning continued as follows:

Q: So if you were watching outside the front wall, that front wall faces the hide-site, is that correct?

---

29   "Costello: Well, then, who's on first.
Abbott: Yes.
I mean the fellow's name.
Who.
The guy on first.
Who.
The first baseman.
Who.
The guy playing...
Who is on first!
I'm asking YOU who's on first…"

A: Which front wall?

Q: The wall that you are looking out of?

A: No. The wall behind me.

Q: Is open? The wall behind you?

A: No, the wall behind me has the hide-site behind me.

Q: Roger. And you don't remember if you were in the prone or sitting or?

A: No, not really.

At this point, the male prosecutor, who was visibly frustrated, interjected and took over the questioning, asking Redfern to draw a detailed map outlining the location and position of the pump house as well as the rest of the snipers. Redfern complied. (That drawing is shown in the middle section of this book.) After a number of additional succinct and direct questions from the male prosecutor clearly outlining on the map where everyone was located on 11 May, questioning by the original prosecutor resumed:

Q; Sergeant Redfern, what kind of training have you received on the treatment of detainees?

A: I don't know. Detain them.

Q: What about what you're supposed to do with them while they are detained?

A: Not sure.

Q: You've received training on that?

A: METT-TC[30], it's dependent upon the situation what you do...

---

30   METT-TC is the acronym for factors that commanders and individual soldiers use to assess a battle space or a specific engagement. The factors include the mission, enemy, terrain and weather, troops and support available, time available, and civil considerations.

The questioning continued, as follows:

Q: Did you ever receive a class on the Law of War?

A: Probably.

Q: In your sworn statement to CID, you said that you discussed what had gone on at the 11 May incident with Sandoval at some length?

A: No, I said it might have been Sandoval that I discussed it with.

Q: You did actually say that it was Sandoval in your statement. Would you like to review your statement?

A: Sure. [Prosecutor looked for the appropriate statement.]

Q: I'm showing you page five of seven of your statement. [Prosecutor handed the statement to Redfern.] Look about halfway down the page. [Redfern did as directed.]

A: Okay. [Redfern returned the statement to the prosecutor.]

Q: And do you recall answering a question that: "What was the discussion that you and Specialist Sandoval had?"

A: I said it was wrong.

Q: Say again?

A: I said it was wrong.

Q: Yes?

A: All right, yeah.

Q: Okay. What made you think that was wrong?

A: Something seemed out of place, but like I said before, the reason I didn't come forward was there wasn't enough information.

Q: It seemed wrong to you? You said something. What was wrong about this incident is what you were asked in this statement and you responded, "It is not right to murder people."

A: Yeah.

Q: And then in this next question, "Do you feel that in this incident that the Iraqi male was murdered?" And you responded, "Yes, because unless the guy had been released and came back with a weapon that is the only other answer." Is that correct? Yes or no?

A: Yes.

Q: The next question was, "Was the scenario of the Iraqi male being released and returning at all feasible?" And you said, "No, it is not, it is really not." Is that correct?

A: Yeah, that was then, but that was before I had other information.

Q: Understood—

A: Exactly what—

Q: At the time—

A: …SGT Hand could see so, yes, during that specific time, yes, that's what I thought.

Q: Okay and you and Sandoval were talking about going to the Battalion Commander, is that correct?

A: I don't know if it was the Battalion Commander.

Q: That's what you said in your statement.

A: Possibly.

Q: Yes.

A: Okay, yeah, either that or the chaplain.

Q: Okay, but neither of you did, is that correct?

A: No.

Q: Did you talk to SGT Hand? Did you talk to him? What were you talking about when you just said, a moment ago, that you had more information based on Sergeant Hand?

A: What Sergeant Hand could see and he couldn't see back to the backside like that.

Q: So that changed your opinion somehow?

A: Yeah.

Q: How so?

A: Because if you have a blank area in your vision, you're not going to see someone coming from that side.

Q: Okay.

A: So it is possible.

Q: You detained the guy, correct? You detained this individual when he came into the hide-site?

A: Yep.

Q: Yes. You put a poncho over his head?

A: Yep.

Q: You searched him?

A: Yes.

Q: He didn't have an AK-47 on him?

A: Nope.

Q: Was that the same guy that you saw lying in the hide-site?

A: Like I said, I don't know. Possibly, maybe.

Q: Possibly, maybe? You saw the guy?

A: As I was waking up, yeah, and I couldn't really tell you what the guy was wearing, what the guy looked like. Only knew that he was Iraqi.

Q: And he had an AK-47 on him?

A: Yep. The detainee or the dead guy?

Q: The dead guy.

A: Yeah.

Q: You stated earlier that you probably had some training on Law of War. Do you remember participating in a class or sitting through a class, prior to deployment that was taught by a JAG officer regarding the Law of War?

A: Okay, yeah. At the gym.

Q: At the gym?

A: Yes.

Q: And that occurred before you deployed?

[Redfern nodded.]

Q: And what do you remember about that as it relates to detainees? Well, what's your understanding of when you detain someone, how you are supposed to treat them?

A: As a human being.

Q: Describe a little bit more, as a human being, what do you mean by that?

A: Safeguard them.

Q: Protect them? Protect them from harm? Now granted, if they walk into your hide-site, sure, you have to detain them. It's not unreasonable to blindfold. It's not unreasonable to tie them up, is that correct?

A: It's perfectly legitimate.

Q: When a detainee is bound and blindfolded, is it acceptable to beat that detainee?

[Redfern nodded giving a negative response.]

Q: Is it acceptable to shoot that detainee?

A: No.

Q: Was there anything between the pump house and the hide-site that blocked your vision? I understand that you drew a wall here [pointing at the map Redfern had drawn]. I got that, was there anything else in between? Did you hear anything from the hide-site?

A: What do you mean?

Q: Did you hear the detainee? Did you hear him cry?

A: No.

Q: Did you hear him make any noise?

A: He may have said that he was hot. I don't know. I think he said that he was hot.

Q: Now was that while you were in the pump house?

A: No, that was right as I was getting up to go and talk to Sergeant Hand.

Q: While you were in the pump house, did you hear anything from the hide-site, other than the two shots? Did you hear any conversations? Did you hear the detainee cry? Did you hear anything?

A: No.

Q: So you didn't hear Staff Sergeant Hensley saying anything?

A: No.

Q: So you didn't hear Sergeant Vela say anything?

A: No.

Q: Did Sandoval leave the pump house when he was with you?

A: Yeah, after the shots were fired.

Q: But in between the time that you came into the pump house and he left because of the shots?

A: Nope.

Q: Did you say anything to Sergeant Vela after you heard the shots and went back to the hide-site?

A: Nope.

Q: You didn't say a word?

A: I don't know.

Q: You don't remember? When you went back to the hide-site, what happened at that point?

A: I grabbed my gear and headed back to the pump house.

Q: Who was with you at that point?

A: Sandoval.

Q: So you and Sandoval went back to the hide-site?

A: Hide-site, yes.

Q: What did you do once you got back to the hide-site?

A: Continued to pull security in case anyone rolled up on us.

Q: Did you see the body?

A: Yeah, for like three seconds.

Q: And you didn't have any reaction to it?

A: No. All's I saw was an AK. That was all I needed. Besides that, there's more important things than a dead guy on the ground when he has possible friends that are going to come and roll up on us. The last concern is a dead body.

Q: How was Staff Sergeant Hensley reacting?

A: I don't know, like Staff Sergeant Hensley.

Q: How about Sergeant Vela?

A: He looked weird.

Q: What about Specialist Sandoval?

A: I don't know. I think he said, "Are we getting out of here now? Is someone on the way?"

Q: What happened next?

A: Staff Sergeant Hensley threw purple smoke. SSE showed up. We rolled out. And walked back with helicopters covering us.

Q: When you say Sergeant Vela looked weird, what do you mean by weird? Can you describe what was weird?

A: He just killed a person. How would you feel after you killed someone?

Q: Did he look upset?

A: No, he looked like he had just killed a person for the first time.

Q: Can you describe how a person who's killed a person for the first time would look?

Redfern responded to this question by glaring at the prosecutor and not saying a word. He clearly did not like the question. After a long pause, Redfern answered:

A: ...Not really. Just messed up from it. How would you feel if you had to shoot someone?

Q: Thank you, Sergeant Redfern.

Sergeant Redfern then responded to my cross-examination. I introduced myself, exchanged pleasantries, and then handed him the Geronimo Mission Patrol Brief that Didier had testified about and asked him to glance through it.

Q: Now, do you recognize this thing?

A: No.

Q: Did you receive a brief, like this, before every mission you did?

A: No.

Q: So Captain Didier didn't bring you all in and pull out this book and walk through a brief like this before every mission?

A: No, he didn't.

Q: Now regarding these deployment briefings on the Law of War, back in Alaska, you said you remember that you went to some Law of War briefing back in Alaska, right?

A: Yeah, I think it was involved with all of the medical stuff as well.

Q: About how many briefings would you say that you received back in Alaska, prior to deploying?

A: I can tell you that day was probably about four hours plus the briefings.

Q: And this was just one of the many briefings?

A: Yes.

Q: Have you received any follow-on briefings on the Law of War at Iskandariyah or in country?

A: Yeah, after the murder trials started.

Q: But not before?

A: I don't think so.

Q: And you talked about detaining people and you used the term, METT-T, and that's, you know, Mission, Enemy, Terrain, Time, Troops Available.

A: Yep.

Q: And in some situations, when you're in a hide-site, you are somewhat hiding, correct?

A: Yes.

Q: And it's important that if you are detaining somebody that sometimes you silence them, correct?

A: Yeah.

Q: And in some situations you have to be more aggressive than others in silencing somebody, correct?

A: Yes.

Q: And just so we're clear, there's been a lot of discussion about the pump house—I thought we were going to rebuild the thing here—but I just want to make it very crystal clear, Specialist Sandoval was in the pump house at the time that this person was shot, correct?

A: Roger that. He was a foot away from me.

Q: Okay. And that's 25 to 30 meters away from where this person was killed, correct?

A: Roger that. Roughly about that distance.

Q: And you all were on security, looking outward, correct?

A: Roger.

Q: And you never saw Specialist Sandoval place an AK-47 on this person, did you?

A: No.

Q: Okay. And you never heard any conversation with Sergeant Vela and Specialist Sandoval, "Hey, let's come up with a plan and kill this person." Correct?

A: Negative.

Q: Okay. Are you aware that Specialist Sandoval has been charged with the premeditated murder of this guy?

A: Of this guy?

Q: Yep.

A: No, I didn't know that.

Q: Are you aware that they've charged him with placing an AK-47 on this person's remains?

A: No, I did not know.

Q: Do you believe, based upon your experience being there, that Specialist Sandoval either placed an AK-47 on him or had anything at all to do...

At this point the prosecutors stood up and loudly objected to the question. A long exchange with the investigating officer began with the prosecutors objecting to my question based on various legal arguments about how my questioning was improper because they did not have to prove that Sandoval himself placed the AK-47 on the deceased person in order to gain a conviction. However, Major Hasse quickly shot the prosecutors down and ruled that my questions were proper.

My questioning continued, as follows:

Q: Do you believe that there is any evidence that you know of to support the charge that Specialist Sandoval murdered Genei Nesir Khudair Al-Janabi?

A: No.

Q: And do you know of anything that he did regarding placing an AK-47 on this person's remains?

A: Unless he miracled it there, no.

Q: Okay. Now there was an issue about you and Specialist Sandoval not reporting this murder, correct?

A: Roger that.

Q: You made some statements about that, correct?

A: Yeah, roger that. I'm currently flagged because of it...

Redfern and all the other snipers present on 11 May had been "flagged" since the murder allegations broke. Flagging is the process of stopping any positive actions such as promotions or awards because the soldier is under investigation.

My questioning continued, as follows:

Q: And one of the reasons in your discussions with Specialist Sandoval, why you didn't report it, is one: you didn't know for sure what had happened in that hide-site, correct?

A. Roger that.

Q: And two: you were scared of possible repercussions, is that correct?

A: Roger that, it is. If you don't have 100 percent evidence, you don't go and accuse someone, "Hey, you murdered someone." Because stuff like this happens. And I'm not about ruining someone's life over something I don't know—that I don't have complete evidence on. Now if I did have complete, 100 percent evidence, I'd say, "Roger that. This person did this."

Q: In fact, in this case, you've been told all sorts of different things, by all sorts of different people, correct?

A: Roger that.

Q: CID told you one thing, correct?

A: Yeah.

Q: And then you've heard other things, correct? And those aren't always the same, right?

A: No, you have CID and then you have the truth.

This last statement by Redfern was simple, yet it captured the essence of the case. It had become evident that Sandoval and I wanted the truth to shine through, whereas the prosecutors and CID appeared to only want a conviction. Major Hasse then had some final questions for Redfern. He revisited the issue of the Geronimo Mission Patrol Brief and whether or not Redfern and the team had been briefed and how extensively. Redfern's answers were consistent with his previous testimony. Hasse then confirmed that Redfern and the team had dealt with detainees before and never had any issues regarding their treatment of them or complaints afterward. He then continued his questioning of Redfern, as follows:

Q: Back to the shooting. How much time between the two shots and you popping your head out of the pump house? Was that like immediate, or as immediate as possible?

A: Yeah, as immediate as possible.

Q: Okay. Did you even look into the hide-site? Or did you just look outside to make sure nothing was happening outside the hide-site?

A: I popped my head out, looked like this [Redfern turned his head to the left and right to demonstrate] and took a couple of steps to the left. Saw a guy. Ran back in and said, "Hey Sandoval, get your shit. Get back here, we're leaving. Somebody got killed. I'm grabbing my stuff. We'll wait here until SSE gets here and we'll provide security this way."

Q: And while you were doing that, did you not see an AK? You didn't necessarily note a weapon on the person when you looked at them right away, I imagine, because they were 20 meters away? You just saw someone laying.

A: I heard two shots. Saw Vela with a 9mm. Guy on the ground. Went in and told him to get his stuff. Because, like I said, a dead body is not a real big concern of mine when you're in Jurf as Sakhr.

Q: Right. And then how long until you got back out to the body itself after you guys grabbed your kit?

A: Like meaning when SSE showed up after Staff Sergeant Hensley threw the violet smoke?

Q: I think I misunderstood. So you stayed in the pump house after the shooting and continued to pull security?

A: Yes.

Q: Okay, thanks. And Sandoval stayed there with you?

A: Yeah, roger that."

♦ ♦ ♦

SERGEANT RICHARD HAND

After Sergeant Redfern's testimony, I called Sergeant Richard Hand as our witness. He was home on leave back in the States and was called on the phone for his testimony. Because of the time difference, Hand had been asleep at the time of the call and during his testimony it was clear that he was very tired. After he was sworn in, the prosecutor also read Hand his Article 32 rights. He waived his rights and testified via the phone call to my questions as follows:

(Q: DEFENSE COUNSEL)

(A: SGT HAND)

Q. Sergeant Hand, this is Captain Drummond, how are you doing?

A. I'm doing pretty good, sir.

Q: Probably a little tired. All right, let me just jump into the questions here. Do you recall 11 May 2007?

A: You're going to have to refresh my memory on what we're talking about here, sir.

Q: If I said that was the day that Sergeant Vela allegedly shot somebody, does that ring a bell?

A: Yes, it does.

Q: And where were you at the time that the shooting occurred?

A: When Sergeant Vela shot the guy, that whole day and the day prior I was on a dirt berm, a small little hill.

Q: And do you know where Specialist Sandoval was?

A: I know where I was told he was at, but I can't specifically say where he was or was not at. To the best of my knowledge he was inside of a pump house.

Q: With Sergeant Redfern?

A: That is correct.

Q: At any time on 11 May, or any time before that or after that did you ever see Specialist Sandoval with an AK-47?

A: I did not.

Q: Did you ever see Specialist Sandoval place somebody else's AK-47 on the deceased body on 11 May 2007?

A: I did not.

Q: Did you see Specialist Sandoval have anything at all to do with the murder of that deceased?

A: I did not...

We then established that Hand did not believe he had failed to report the death, but in fact believed that everyone in the battalion knew "that we had killed a guy."

I continued my questioning of Hand, as follows:

Q: At that point in time, right after 11 May, did you believe that you had enough information to think that there was, in fact, a murder, or were you unsure, in fact, there was a murder of that person?

A: At the time, in my opinion, it had not been a murder. I was of the opinion that it was a clean shoot.

Q: And that was with the facts you knew at the time, correct?

A: That is correct.

Q: Did you ever see Specialist Sandoval treat that detainee, before he was shot, did you ever see him treat that detainee inhumanely?

A: I did not.

Q: Have you ever seen Specialist Sandoval treat a detainee inhumanely?

A: I have not.

Q: Now, Sergeant Hand, the government has charged Specialist Sandoval with murdering that detainee on 11 May 2007. Do you know of any evidence to support that charge?

A: No, sir.

Q: The government has charged Specialist Sandoval with placing an AK-47 on the deceased body of that detainee. Do you know of any evidence to support that charge?

A: I do not, sir.

Neither Hasse nor the prosecutors had any questions for Hand and the call was disconnected. At that point, closing arguments were made and at 1144 hours, the hearing closed.

After the close of the hearing, Claudio and I met with Sandoval to recap the testimony and the day. Sandoval was pissed and clearly frustrated. He did not understand how this case, and the charges against him, could continue. I was just as frustrated with the situation as he was and told him not to give up hope. I told Sandoval that I had a renewed faith that Hasse just might do the right thing, and that the prosecutors and command might also reassess their case. Even with my reassurance it was clear that the case was beginning to wear on Sandoval as he was a fighter and wanted to fight, but in the end, he knew that this fight was in my hands and that he could not do much more than sit back, take notes, and watch.

As Claudio and I took a Blackhawk flight back to Anaconda that night, I felt confident that the additional murder charge would be dismissed. After all, there was zero evidence presented that Sandoval had anything to do with the shooting or that he had planted the AK-47.

I thought, *Well, perhaps the inhumane treatment charge or the failure to report the shooting charge will remain, but the murder charge, absolutely not.*

On 20 August, Hasse recommended that the murder charge against Sandoval and the charge of dereliction of duty for not ensuring the humane treatment of the detainee should both be dismissed. He wrote in his report that "all statements and evidence place SPC Sandoval in the pump house, away from the location of the 'close kill'….Sandoval never knew SSG Hensley planned to kill the detainee." This finding by Hasse was a pleasant surprise as it showed that he was not a rubber stamp. Unfortunately, Hasse recommended that charges against Sandoval go forward to general court-martial for failing to report the murder of the detainee and for having something to do with wrongfully placing an AK-47 on the detainee.

I knew that Hasse was just making a non-binding recommendation, but I certainly thought the murder charge would be dismissed because this was the same officer who had recommended that the earlier charges proceed forward. I thought that the command would give some deference to their own investigating officer's opinion. After all, Sandoval was not even present at the location of the shooting, and no one said that he had anything to do with it. However, I was not sure what to think about Hasse's finding related to the remaining charges against Sandoval as it seemed inconsistent. If Sandoval was not present at the 11 May shooting and did not see it, then why should he have reported it as a murder?

Hasse also recommended that charges be preferred against Redfern and Hand for also placing an AK-47 on the detainee and for failing to report the murder. The report and charges were then forwarded to Sandoval's Brigade Commander and then the Commanding General of the 3rd Infantry Division for disposition. While I did not want any additional soldiers charged with crimes, I thought that the recommendation was at least coherent. The 11 May murder charge should be dismissed. If the prosecutors were going to blame Sandoval for anything related to the 11 May incident, then he was not the only one who should be carrying the burden of the charges.

CPT Drummond at the helicopter landing pad at FOB Iskan.

The entrance to FOB Iskan.

SPC Sandoval and CPT Drummond at FOB Iskan for the original Article 32.

Aerial view of the Mussayib power plant on the outskirts of FOB Iskan.

*CPT Claudio, SPC Sandoval and CPT Drummond
at the TDS Defense Office after the trial.*

CPT Drummond trying to grab a little shut-eye while awaiting travel and one of the many airport "lounges" in Iraq.

CPT Drummond traveling in Iraq to meet witnesses carrying maps, exhibits and a box of files.

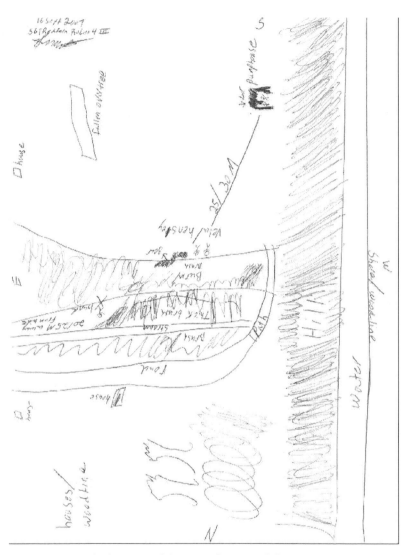

Map the location of the pump house and the geographic area of the 11 May 2006 shooting.

DEPARTMENT OF THE ARMY
HEADQUARTERS, 4TH BRIGADE COMBAT TEAM (ABN),
28TH INFANTRY DIVISION
FOB KALSU, IRAQ
APO AE 09312

REPLY TO
ATTENTION OF:

APVR-ABN-CO   19 July 2007

MEMORANDUM FOR CPT Craig Drummond, Trial Defense Counsel, LSA Anaconda,
Balad, Iraq APO AE 09391

SUBJECT: Request for access to Crime Scene in U.S. v. SPC Jorge G. Sandoval, Jr.

1. I am denying your request at this time for a dedicated security team to provide
access to the crime scene location in the vicinity of Abu Shemsi, Iraq.

2. The area you are requesting to visit is in a very volatile region that is not frequented
by Coalition Forces. Mounted movement to the site is currently not possible due to cuts
in the roads. A dismounted movement of the distance required would place Soldiers at
high risk due to the substantial IED and small arms fire threat in the area. Ultimately, a
mission such as this might require either a dedicated air insertion or a deliberate route
clearance operation. Neither of which do I presently have assets to support.

3. POC is MAJ Richard DiMeglio at ▉▉▉▉▉ or ▉▉▉▉▉▉▉▉▉▉▉.

MICHAEL X. GARRETT
COL, IN
Commanding

Memorandum denying access to the crime scene.

SNIPER TRAINING

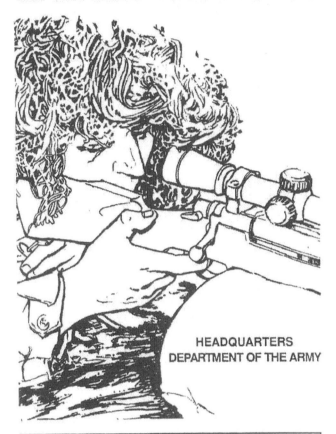

HEADQUARTERS
DEPARTMENT OF THE ARMY

DISTRIBUTION RESTRICTION—
Approved for public release; distribution is unlimited.

The cover of Army Field Manual 23-10.

CHARGE SHEET

I. PERSONAL DATA

1. NAME OF ACCUSED (Last, First, MI)	2. SSN	3. GRADE OR RANK	4. PAY GRADE
SANDOVAL, Jorge G., Jr.	▮▮▮▮▮	SPC	E-4

5. UNIT OR ORGANIZATION	6. CURRENT SERVICE	
	a. INITIAL DATE	b. TERM
Headquarters and Headquarters Company, 1st Battalion, 501st Infantry, Forward Operating Base Iskandariyah, Iraq APO AE 09312-0506	▮▮▮▮▮	42 mo

7. PAY PER MONTH			8. NATURE OF RESTRAINT OF ACCUSED	9. DATE(S) IMPOSED
a. BASIC	b. SEA/FOREIGN DUTY	c. TOTAL	None	N/A
$1,883.10	$100.00	$1,983.10		

II. CHARGES AND SPECIFICATIONS

10. CHARGE I: VIOLATION OF THE UCMJ, ARTICLE 118

THE SPECIFICATION: In that Specialist Jorge G. Sandoval, Jr., did, at or near Abu Shemsi, Iraq, on or about 27 April, 2007, murder an Iraqi national by means of shooting him with a rifle.

CHARGE II: VIOLATION OF THE UCMJ, ARTICLE 134

THE SPECIFICATION: In that Specialist Jorge G. Sandoval, Jr., did, at or near Jurf as Sakhr, Iraq, on or about 11 April 2007, wrongfully place command wire with the remains of Genei Nesir Khudair Al Janabi, which conduct was to the prejudice of good order and discipline in the armed forces or of a nature to bring discredit upon the armed forces.

END OF CHARGES

III. PREFERRAL

11a. NAME OF ACCUSER (Last, First, MI)	b. GRADE	c. ORGANIZATION OF ACCUSER
LEVINE, Charles R.	CPT	HHC, 1st Battalion, 501st Infantry

d. SIGNATURE OF ACCUSER	e. DATE
(signature)	28 JUN 07

AFFIDAVIT: Before me, the undersigned, authorized by law to administer oaths in cases of this character, personally appeared the above named accuser this __88th__ day of __June__, 2007, and signed the foregoing charges and specifications under oath that he/she is a person subject to the Uniform Code of Military Justice and that he/she either has personal knowledge of or has investigated the matters set forth therein and that the same are true to the best of his/her knowledge and belief.

SARAH J. RYKOWSKI	HHC, 4TH BCT (ABN), 25TH ID
Typed Name of Officer	Organization of Officer
CPT	Trial Counsel
Grade	Official Capacity to Administer Oath (See R.C.M. 307(b) – must be a commissioned officer)
(signature)	
Signature	

DD FORM 458, MAY 2000   PREVIOUS EDITION IS OBSOLETE.

The original charges preferred against SPC Sandoval.

CHARGE SHEET

I. PERSONAL DATA

1. NAME OF ACCUSED (Last, First, MI)	2. SSN	3. GRADE OR RANK	4. PAY GRADE
SANDOVAL, Jorge G., Jr.	▮▮▮▮▮	SPC	E-4

5. UNIT OR ORGANIZATION	6. CURRENT SERVICE		
Headquarters and Headquarters Company, 1st Battalion, 501st Infantry, Forward Operating Base Iskandariyah, Iraq APO AE 09312-0506	a. INITIAL DATE ▮▮▮▮	b. TERM 42 mo	

7. PAY PER MONTH			8. NATURE OF RESTRAINT OF ACCUSED	9. DATE(S) IMPOSED
a. BASIC	b. SEA/FOREIGN DUTY	c. TOTAL	Pretrial Confinement	29 Jun 07 - Present
$1,883.10	$100.00	$1,983.10		

II. CHARGES AND SPECIFICATIONS

10. ADDITIONAL CHARGE I: VIOLATION OF THE UCMJ, ARTICLE 118

SPECIFICATION: In that Specialist Jorge G. Sandoval, Jr., U.S. Army, did, at or near Jurf as Sakhr, Iraq, on or about 11 May 2007, with premeditation, murder Genei Nesir Khudair Al-Janabi by means of shooting him with a 9mm pistol.

ADDITIONAL CHARGE II: VIOLATION OF THE UCMJ, ARTICLE 92

SPECIFICATION 1: In that Specialist Jorge G. Sandoval, Jr., U.S. Army, who knew of his duties, at or near Jurf as Sakhr, Iraq, on or about 11 May 2007, was derelict in the performance of those duties in that he failed to ensure the humane treatment of a detainee, as it was his duty to do.

SPECIFICATION 2: In that Specialist Jorge G. Sandoval, Jr., U.S. Army, who knew of his duties, at or near Jurf as Sakhr, Iraq, and at or near Forward Operating Base Iskandariyah, Iraq, from between on or about 11 May 2007 and on or about 27 June 2007, was derelict in the performance of those duties in that he willfully failed to report the murder of a detainee, as it was his duty to do.

ADDITIONAL CHARGE III: VIOLATION OF THE UCMJ, ARTICLE 134

SPECIFICATION: In that Specialist Jorge G. Sandoval, Jr., U.S. Army, did, at or near Jurf as Sakhr, Iraq, on or about 11 May 2007, wrongfully place an AK-47 rifle with the remains of Genei Nesir Khudair Al Janabi, which conduct was to the prejudice of good order and discipline in the armed forces or of a nature to bring discredit upon the armed forces.

END OF ADDITIONAL CHARGES

III. PREFERRAL

11a. NAME OF ACCUSER (Last, First, MI)	b. GRADE	c. ORGANIZATION OF ACCUSER
LEVINE, Charles R.	CPT	HHC, 1ST BN, 501ST IN

d. SIGNATURE OF ACCUSER	e. DATE
[signature]	5 AUG 07

AFFIDAVIT: Before me, the undersigned, authorized by law to administer oaths in cases of this character, personally appeared the above named accuser this ___5th___ day of ___Aug___, 2007, and signed the foregoing charges and specifications under oath that he/she is a person subject to the Uniform Code of Military Justice and that he/she either has personal knowledge of or has investigated the matters set forth therein and that the same are true to the best of his/her knowledge and belief.

JAMES H. YAW	HHC, 1ST BN, 501ST IN
Typed Name of Officer	Organization of Officer
CPT	Adjutant
Grade	Official Capacity to Administer Oath (See R.C.M. 307(b) — must be a commissioned officer)
[signature]	
Signature	

DD FORM 458, MAY 2000   PREVIOUS EDITION IS OBSOLETE.

The additional charges preferred against SPC Sandoval, to include actions related to the 11 May 2007 incident.

TEN - ONWARD TO TRIAL

"The truth is found when men are free to pursue it."

~ Franklin Roosevelt, *Great Quotes from Great Leaders* (Celebrating Excellence Publishing, 1990)

The reopened Article 32 investigation was now behind us and Major General Lynch referred all the charges, including the 11 May 2007 murder charge, to a general court-martial. Bam! The general apparently did not care what Hasse had to say about 11 May. Sandoval was to stand trial on all charges, regardless of Hasse's recommendation for dismissal. It was clear that the prosecution was trying to hammer Sandoval with everything they could.

Referring the case to a general court-martial is sending the case to the highest level court where the soldier faces that harshest potential punishment that exists under the UCMJ. MG Lynch had signed a memorandum referring all the charges to a set panel of soldiers to listen to the evidence and serve as the jury. It would be up to a military panel to decide Sandoval's fate. This action meant that we needed to "suit up" and get ready for a courtroom battle.

The trial was set to take place at the courtroom at Camp Liberty, the large U.S. military base just outside of Baghdad where the reopened Article 32 took place. The courthouse was located adjacent to a large mosque that had once been under Saddam's rule and served as the home of the mosque's imam.[31] At one time it was a beautiful home with a man-made lake in the back. However, the building had been severely vandalized and looted during Saddam's fall.

In its efforts to transform the building into a courthouse,

---

31   An imam is the worship leader and head of a Muslim mosque.

the U.S. Army had jerry-rigged electrical wiring to provide electricity and covered shattered windows with plywood. It was not a pretty sight but it had all the necessities for a trial—a raised bench for the judge, a cordoned-off area for the panel, counsel tables, a gallery with seats for spectators, and an American flag. At the time of the trial, various areas of the Camp Liberty compound received mortar and rocket attacks daily. On the one hand, this was not an ideal environment for trying a case. However, certain aspects of it were perfect for our defense.

Considering that the panel was made up of soldiers who were also serving in Iraq, I wanted to get as close as possible to challenging their own thinking about what they would do and how they would like to be judged if facing a murder charge for actions on the field of battle. There certainly was no better place to accomplish this than in a courthouse located in the heart of a war zone, where the trial would be interrupted by sirens blaring every few hours, alerting the base to an incoming rocket or mortar attack.

In a trial, it is improper to directly ask jury members to place themselves in the shoes of the accused and judge his actions based on what they would do. This is sometimes referred to as "the Golden Rule." However, there is nothing wrong with presenting evidence in such a way that you can get a panel to identify with an accused and see the evidence from his point of view.

The terrifying aspect of Sandoval's case was not necessarily that his future was in my hands, but rather that it was in the hands of others—the panel and possibly the judge. Of course, their decision would be based, at least in part, on the evidence as I portrayed it but at the end of the day, no matter how hard a defense attorney prepares, advocates, or argues, the ultimate decision of guilt or innocence is not his to make.

As this was a general court-martial, Sandoval had

the option of being tried by military judge alone, a panel comprised of all officers, or a panel of two-thirds officers and one-third enlisted members. The decision as to the composition of who can sit as a panel member is initially made by the commanding general—in this case, Major General (MG) Rick Lynch, Commander of the 3rd Infantry Division.[32] The General is supposed to select officers and enlisted members based on "age, experience, education, training, length of service, and judicial temperament."

Normally, a panel is selected in twelve-person increments and when a court-martial begins, all twelve selected are required to appear. Just as in a civilian jury trial, before the trial begins, the judge, trial counsel, and defense have the opportunity to ask questions of the members to ensure that they will be impartial and fair. This is the *voir dire* process. The required quorum for a general court-martial is five members. Thus, at least five members must remain after questioning for the court to be assembled and the trial to commence. If there are less than five members, the General selects additional panel members as needed.

We wanted a panel of soldiers as close to the actual ground warfighting in Iraq as possible, so Sandoval elected to have a panel with at least one-third enlisted members. Picking the best jury for a case is a byzantine task. There are probably fifty books written about jury selection, as well as numerous psychologists, social workers, and consultants with businesses that revolve around assisting attorneys with just picking a jury. We did not have the pleasure of a jury consultant or other assistance, so Claudio and I had to rely on our own experience and intuition in hopefully seating the

---

32   The 3rd Infantry Division was based out of Fort Stewart, Georgia. The division deployed to Iraq in March of 2007 and took over the command of Multinational Forces Iraq-Center (MNF-C). Sandoval's unit fell under MNF-C for court-martial jurisdiction. As such, MG Lynch was the General ultimately responsible for the investigation, prosecution, and court-martial of Sandoval.

fairest jury possible. We discussed all of Sandoval's options about having just military officers or also having enlisted members on the panel, and we chose to also have enlisted members present.

Sandoval was a young infantryman who had been placed in many difficult positions that led to his trial. He was following a direct order on 27 April and then did not question the actions of senior enlisted members about the 11 May incident. It was our belief that an enlisted member would be able to relate more to Sandoval's actions, rather than an officer who may have never been the lowest ranking soldier on a mission. We wanted someone to agree that given all of the circumstances that Sandoval, a Specialist in the Army, made appropriate and reasonable actions for a man of his age and rank.

Twelve soldiers had been selected, and we went through the *voir dire* process with seven soldiers ultimately remaining. The panel members who were seated included a Lieutenant Colonel, Major, Captain, Sergeant Major, Master Sergeant, Sergeant First Class, and a Staff Sergeant, which meant that we had more than one-third enlisted members who would ultimately decide Sandoval's fate.

◆ ◆ ◆

One day before the court-martial convened for a pretrial session, the waters were muddied when, on 24 September 2007, *The Washington Post* published an article on the front page titled, "U.S. Aims to Lure Insurgents with Bait." The article was penned by two *Washington Post* staff writers and stated, "A Pentagon group has encouraged some U.S. military snipers in Iraq to target suspected insurgents by scattering pieces of 'bait,' such as detonation cords, plastic explosives and ammunition, and then killing Iraqis who pick up the items, according to military court documents.

"The classified program was described in investigative documents related to recently filed murder charges against three snipers who are accused of planting evidence on Iraqis they killed…"

CPT Didier was quoted in the article, specifically citing a sworn statement that he made during the course of the murder investigations as follows: "'Baiting is putting an object out there that we know they will use, with the intention of destroying the enemy,' Capt. Matthew P. Didier, the leader of an elite sniper scout platoon attached to the 1st Battalion of the 501st Infantry Regiment, said in a sworn statement. 'Basically, we would put an item out there and watch it. If someone found the item, picked it up, and attempted to leave with the item, we would engage the individual as I saw this as a sign they would use the item against U.S. Forces…'"

The article relied on evidence obtained by reporters from family members of the soldiers allegedly involved in the baiting.

The next day—the same day the pretrial session was convened—*The New York Times* also broke an article from its own sources about the same baiting practices.

I was not surprised by the stories. Because I felt that the prosecution of Sandoval represented an injustice, I had been in contact with the media and was discussing the case with one of the reporters from the *Post* who was covering the war from Baghdad. Our conversations involved me advocating to the reporter my belief that the American public needed to know that an innocent soldier was standing trial for murder for doing his job in Iraq. This was in direct response to the original press releases issued by the military public affairs office of the command. My command within the JAG Corps was aware that I was talking with the press, and I had sought out their guidance on the rights-and-lefts of dealing with the media. While they did not encourage me to talk to the press, they understood why I did it, and as long as I followed their guidance agreed to have my back should any repercussions follow from publicly disagreeing with the prosecution of Sandoval. Being independent from the local command is one of the great traditions about being a defense attorney under the U.S. Army Trial Defense Service.[33] I did not report to anyone in Sandoval's chain of command and if necessary was free to challenge, question, and criticize the command of soldiers whom I was defending.

I had not discussed the specific allegation of baiting or any similar tactic with this reporter or any other reporter. However, I was aware that both the *Post* and the *Times* had been provided some evidence in the cases from other sources and were planning on writing about the baiting concept.

My initial reaction to the baiting headlines was that it was not good for Sandoval as it confused his case. While there certainly may have been questionable programs occurring with his unit's and other unit's missions in the Iskandariyah area, classified and unclassified, the fact was that Sandoval was not a part of them. Sandoval's case did not appear to directly involve any program or mission to plant weapons on dead bodies or to bait and shoot.

Many of the newspaper articles about the case also dealt with soldiers stating that their command pressured them to get more kills. However, from my point of view, all the allegations about baiting and pushing kills were potential defenses but they were not what Sandoval's case was about.

It is true that a desire for more kills was pushed down from both Sandoval's battalion commander and higher-ups. There was also strong evidence that the battalion commander and

---

33   The U.S. Army Trial Defense Service (TDS) was formally created in 1980 as an independent "Field Operating Agency" and is a separate command solely for Army defense counsel. The senior command of TDS report directly to an office in Fort Belvoir, Virginia, and their independence from local command influence is intrepidly protected by the senior officers in the JAG Corps.

command Sergeant Major had insinuated that the unit should get more kills and be less restrictive about determining when to fire. The command emphasized more kills because they were taking heavy casualties and had previously bounded their own troops by briefing the Rules of Engagement in vague and overreaching terms.

However, when I looked at the actions of 27 April 2007, I could see nothing wrong regardless of whether the desire for kills was pushed down or not. Our defense argument was that the deceased was an insurgent who had attacked U.S. troops, plain and simple. The push for more kills may have been a partial motivator for Didier to authorize Hensley for the shooting, but in the end, it was a justified kill. There was no need to assign blame at the senior leadership of Sandoval's unit when in the end what happened was legitimate.

Throughout the case, there were other attorneys and some members of Sandoval's unit who questioned why in the defense of Sandoval we did not bring up the baiting issue or the issue of the command pushing the younger soldiers for more kills. Potentially, such activities could serve as a powerful defense. I understood their skepticism. However, in making my decision I had been briefed formally and informally about all the tactics, classified and unclassified, that Sandoval's unit was employing in their missions—or, at least we were *told* that we had been briefed about all the tactics and programs. In addition to the briefings I knew from Sandoval which tactics he was, and was not, aware of and what specific programs that he did and did not participate in. Given all of this, Claudio and I made the tactical decision not to get into classified areas and not to try and shift the blame onto the chain of command about pushing kills.

Classified evidence creates a complicated case that breaks up a trial into choppy sections between the unclassified parts that are public and the classified portions that are private behind closed doors. It was not, however, the mechanics of doing a classified case that ultimately caused us to avoid going into that evidence. Rather, Claudio and I felt that the evidence would have clouded our case and our overall theme and defense strategy.

To allege that the command was pushing kills in turn alleges that the shooting of 27 April was pushed from higher-ups and was unnecessary or without justification, and hence illegitimate. It was our position that nothing was illegitimate about the shooting. Thus, it would run contrary to our strategy if we decided to bring forth evidence that insinuated that the shooting itself was unnecessary or without justification.

The baiting issue was more complicated because there were real questions about command implemented programs in Sandoval's case about planting evidence—namely the command wire on 27 April and the AK-47 on 11 May. However, even if such an evidence-planting program existed and was implemented, the fact is that the government had not charged Sandoval with baiting. They had charged him with placing an item on the body of an already deceased person. To bring up the baiting issue would ultimately cause a distraction from our defense strategy of complete innocence. It is true that the allegation that the unit authorized the planting of certain types of items could support a "mistake of fact" defense as to whether Sandoval was mistaken as to whether the planting of command wire on a deceased was wrongful or done with authorization.

However, in the end, evidence or arguments about any sort of baiting program could also cause a panel to question everything that Sandoval's unit was doing. If the panel began to question every action of the unit, then they could also start to question the legitimacy of the shooting of 27 April and so forth. Thus, introducing the baiting issue as a defense created a slippery slope, one which we tactically chose not to traverse.

It has been my experience that a well-tried case, whether

you're prosecuting or defending, revolves around a simple straightforward theme. To allege and present alternative theories to a panel clouds the case and often fails. A jury does not like to hear, "Well, this is what happened, but if you do not believe this is what happened then consider that it also could have happened this other way."

Presenting alternative theories to a jury at trial might be a sound strategy in a contract case or certain types of civil lawsuits. However, when dealing with a criminal case where you are trying to cast reasonable doubt on the prosecution's case by providing a clear them and complete defense, a waffling strategy is normally a failing one.

◆ ◆ ◆

On 25 September, the court-martial convened for a pretrial session. The military judge detailed the case was Lieutenant Colonel Michael Hargis, a West Point graduate who attended law school at Notre Dame. He was normally assigned to Germany where he presided over the trials of soldiers stationed there, but had just recently arrived in Iraq for a month-long tour. I had never practiced in front of him and knew little about him. The rumors I had heard was that he tended to favor the prosecution side of cases as a "law and order" type judge, but that he was also fair and mild-tempered. Both rumors would prove to be true during the trial.

Prior to any criminal or civil trial, motions are filed as a mechanism for resolving issues in the case. It has been my experience that there are generally at least two or three motions filed by the defense in most contested cases. Most experienced trial attorneys consider most stock pretrial motions to be frivolous. Stock motions are those that raise general arguments and are not specifically tailored to the facts of that individual case. Some attorneys, both prosecutors and defense counsel, regularly file a litany of stock motions in every case believing that this somehow helps their cause and makes it seem like they have done a lot of work on the case. I do not take this approach. Instead, the limited motions I filed raised some of the real legal issues in the case. The judge's rulings on the motions would play a key part of our defense as we continued to prepare for trial.

By the time of the court-martial, I had already filed the following pretrial motions, which had been ruled upon as follows:

- Motion to Release from Pretrial Confinement
- Outcome: Denied
- Motion to Dismiss for a Violation of Constitutional Right (Self-incrimination issues based on a charge of Sandoval not reporting a crime that he was also charged with committing).
- Outcome: The judge dismissed the failure to report charge.
- Motion to Dismiss for Unreasonable Multiplication of Charges (Charging inhumane treatment for a killing and also the killing, essentially double-charging).
- Outcome: The judge denied the motion pretrial, but held that the accused could not be convicted of both the killing and inhumane treatment and would dismiss one post-trial if convicted of both by the panel.
- Motion to Compel (Trying to get the government to provide certain evidence and witnesses.)
- Outcome: Granted and all witnesses and evidence ordered to be produced for trial.
- Motion for Additional Peremptory Challenges

of Panel Members
- Outcome: Denied
- Motion for Additional Panel Member Questionnaire
- Outcome: Denied
- Motion for Increased Panel Size (Trying to increase the size of the jury selection pool.)
- Outcome: Denied
- Motion for Judicial Notice of Certain Facts (Asking the Court to agree that certain military regulations can be admitted at trial.)
- Outcome: Granted
- Motion for Expert Assistance (Sniper Expert)
- Outcome: Granted
- Motion for Article 13 Credit (Done orally for sentencing credit for Sandoval doing work details and not being permitted to wear his rank at the confinement facility)
- Outcome: Granted ten days credit for not allowing him to wear his rank.

During pretrial there were a number of issues discussed regarding witnesses, discovery, etc. One issue addressed pretrial was the government's motion to exclude any testimony from Didier to the fact that after the shooting on 27 April, he learned that the body was identified as an enemy insurgent—likely the very insurgent that had attacked his unit earlier in the morning.

The government's argument went as follows:

Sir, the government wishes to exclude any evidence regarding the post-mortem identification of the victim on 27 April as an insurgent or a "squirter." And also any information about the discovery, or the location, or the contents of any weapons cache found in that area on that day. Sir, neither of these items, neither of these bits of information refute any of the elements of the offenses charged. They were found after the fact and, in fact, the accused could not possibly have known about the cache, because it wasn't found until after he killed this individual and potentially, as the government has charged him, murdered this individual.

Again, sir, the evidence was not known to the accused at the time he committed these offenses and therefore it's really not legally or logically relevant as to his state of mind or the justification. It's basically information the accused may seek to admit to, after the fact, to justify what he has done. And if we do that, sir, if we allow this information to come in when it wasn't even known to the accused at the time he committed these offenses then we have just created a defense for any other soldier in any other situation to say, "Well, there was a cache found there and, you know, potentially there was a connection," but there is not a reasonably certain connection. Basically they can use any cache in the area to justify whatever they have done, or in this case any identification after the fact to say, "Well, this guy was a bad guy." And, sir, this guy was a bad guy, that fact or—may have been, is not—basically does not affect the intent element of this charge. It does not affect any sort of justification defense or even mistake of fact. If you don't know the facts, sir, you can't be mistaken as to it.

The military judge responded as follows:

Aren't you skipping a step? Not to argue the defense's case for them, but aren't they likely to argue a two-step process: First, that this person was in fact an enemy combatant, therefore, there was a justification…

TC: Roger, sir.

Judge: With no mistake of fact at all.

TC: Roger, sir.

Judge: That it was in fact. And then, if he wasn't an enemy combatant, then there was a mistake of fact. So don't you see that evidence as relevant to whether or not he was an enemy combatant?

It was clear that the military judge did not like the prosecutor's arguments. The prosecutor and judge continued back and forth for a while, and after what seemed like an eternity of just sitting on my seat waiting to stand up and argue, the judge said, "Defense counsel, you may argue."

I outlined a number of arguments in response to the government's intriguing position. One had to do with the fact that if we are talking about who was the enemy, then it is important if we later learned that it was in fact the enemy. For example:

If somebody goes out and kills Bin Laden, the fact that [the person was] Bin Laden is something that was important. The same way if somebody, one of those security guards at the DFAC[34] here in country, shoots somebody walking up to them because they think that person has a bomb on them. They shoot and they kill [that person].

If we later determine that they had a bomb on them, wouldn't we want that information to come out? Or do we say, "Well, wait a minute. We need to look in isolation at what you knew at the time that that person was approaching you and why you took the shot?" No. We look to see if that person was the enemy and that's looking at all of the circumstances.

It also goes into explaining the accused's actions on May 11th. We understand that the government and the way

---

34   DFAC is the term for a U.S. military dining hall. In Iraq the DFAC's were guarded by civilian contractors stationed at the entrances armed with M-16s. Their role was to check the ID's of those entering and to watch for suicide bombers or other individuals seeking to do harm to the large amount of U.S. troops gathered in one location to eat.

they have proceeded, as I've outlined in my brief during the Article 32s, is that the accused should have known that this killing of 27 April was bad; that there was something wrongful about that; and therefore, because Sandoval would have had that knowledge on him when he walked into 11 May, he should have known that these people were doing things that were wrong.

That has been a theory that the government has proceeded upon during pretrial investigations in this case. And at the end of the day, as you heard from Captain Didier, that everybody determined that the 27 April shooting was good, then that is relevant to explain the accused's actions on 11 May. If the accused had no reason to believe that there was anything wrong on 27 April, then the accused should have no notice that there was something wrong—would have no notice that there was something wrong, therefore, he would have no notice to take any other action than to follow the orders of Staff Sergeant Hensley and to follow the directions of Staff Sergeant Hensley and not question what was happening on that day on 11 May."

The judge asked both the government and me numerous additional questions. He then ruled that Didier's testimony and the identification of the Iraqi's body as an insurgent was relevant and admissible.

In a rather large setback, the Judge also ruled that the order given by Captain Didier on 27 April was unlawful. This was a huge problem. and the rationale for the decision was unclear. The determination of the lawfulness of an order is a question of law and up to the judge. Thus, the military panel was going to be instructed at the close of the case that the order was unlawful. In countering this decision, we were only going to be able to argue that there was no way that Sandoval would have thought, or known, that the order was unlawful.[35]

Another issue discussed was that of classified evidence. The government had appointed a military intelligence officer to be present at the case. This officer was to provide any guidance and answer any questions should any classified evidence come out. I had agreed on the record that I did not plan to elicit any classified evidence. Should the government or the intelligence officer believe classified evidence was coming out at trial, then we were going to break, clear the courtroom, and discuss the issue in a closed session, thus making that portion of the trial and any subsequent transcript also classified.

Another item addressed pretrial was the government's inability to produce Sandoval's sister, Ms. Norma Vasquez, as a defense witness. At the motions hearing, the judge ordered the government to produce her live in Iraq as her testimony was relevant and necessary both on the merits and at sentencing in the defense's case. We previously argued that "her personal contact with her brother gives her the unique ability to testify as to his character for truthfulness and his character for peacefulness." In addition we requested her as a sentencing witness "to testify as to her brother's particular acts of good conduct throughout growing up, bravery throughout his life, and evidence of his temperament and his significant rehabilitative potential."

At the end of the day the Judge agreed that if Sandoval was going to face the possibility of the rest of his life in prison that the panel should at least be able to hear testimony directly from a member of his family when considering the appropriate punishment.

After being ordered to produce her live at trial, the government had flown Norma from her home in Laredo,

---

35   Detailed analysis regarding the lawfulness of this order is outlined toward the end of the book. For purposes of the trial, it is noteworthy that this was a huge setback in our defense of Sandoval's actions.

Texas, to Germany and then to Kuwait. The Kuwait customs officials, however, would not let her leave the airport. They detained her for numerous hours because her passport showed her to be a Mexican national. Apparently Mexicans cannot enter Kuwait. This was news to all. Ms. Vasquez had a letter from the United States government requesting that she be allowed entry so that she could be flown by military aircraft into Iraq. She was detained for hours and ultimately placed on a flight back to Germany by the Kuwait government.

At the time of the hearing, Norma was sitting in a German airport awaiting instructions as to whether to return home or try again. Judge Hargis ordered that she be produced and directed the government to exhaust all resources to get her live at trial. We were ultimately notified that the Kuwait officials would not let her enter the country and that it would take the U.S. State Department to intervene to "possibly" have the matter resolved given that she had a Mexican passport. We ultimately decided to proceed forward with the trial instead of continuing to wait days or weeks for Norma to eventually be allowed into Kuwait so that she could then be flown to Iraq. As the trial began, Norma was on a flight back home to Texas.

Sandoval recalls, "I was afforded time to call home every day but sometimes it was only about ten minutes. I would have to talk to someone to let out my emotions. I was mostly in contact with Norma. She was my oldest sister, and I was close with her always. I would talk to her and tell her to tell our parents that I said hi, that they were treating me okay and I was fine.

"My family was very concerned about me. I don't know what was going through their minds, but I know they were really worried. I tried to call and let them know that everything would be okay. Whatever happened, I didn't want them to concern themselves. That would have been a messed-up thing to do to my family. So I kept telling them everything would be fine."

ELEVEN - THE TRIAL

"It is forbidden to kill; therefore, all murderers are punished unless they kill in large numbers and to the sound of trumpets."

~ *Voltaire, "War"*

After the panel was selected and the court assembled, the female prosecutor rose and made her opening statement: May it please the court. There are two questions you will need to answer at the end of this case. One, what was in the accused's, Specialist Sandoval's, mind on 27 April 2007 when he murdered a man who was cutting grass? Two, where was the accused on 11 May 2007 when he aided, abetted, and assisted in the murder of Genei Nesir Khudair Al Janabi, a detainee, with a 9mm pistol from six inches away?

We represent the government in the case against the accused, Specialist Jorge G. Sandoval Jr. At the close of the evidence in this case you will know what the accused was thinking on 27 April 2007 when he murdered that man.

How will you know? Because the evidence will show you that all the man was doing that day was cutting grass. He didn't act in any way hostile. He didn't exhibit any hostile intent toward the accused. He didn't have a weapon, and the accused, you will hear, placed command wire on the body of the man on 27 April 2007.

Turning to 11 May 2007, how will you know that the accused was there aiding, abetting, assisting? You will hear that he told Specialist Hugo Barragan exactly what happened that day. He told the accused that a little boy walked in to the hide-site; that that little boy pointed at the victim. Sandoval saw the little boy point at the victim and say "Father, father." That Sandoval told Specialist Barragan that he heard Staff

Sergeant Hensley say, "Are you ready to do this," and that that Sergeant Vela then shot the man.

You will hear from Specialist Barragan that Specialist Sandoval told him each one of those things. Specialist Barragan will tell you exactly what Specialist Sandoval's reaction was when he told Specialist Barragan what happened.

You will also hear that he told Specialist Alexander Flores what happened that day. That it was the accused who told Sergeant Vela to point his 9mm at Genei Nesir Khudair Al Janabi and detain him. You will hear from Specialist Flores that Specialist Sandoval described Vela's face as he was ordered to take the shot and as he took the shoot. That as he described this the man reacted, the man was sobbing and crying, and that he knew he was going to die.

You will hear most importantly that Specialist Sandoval told Specialist Flores that Sergeant Vela took a long pause when Staff Sergeant Hensley told him to take the shot and he took the shot. You will also hear from Specialist Flores that Specialist Sandoval told him Sergeant Hensley got the AK-47 and threw it on the ground. His own sworn statement will show you that he knows an AK-47 was placed by Genei Nesir Khudair Al Janabi.

You will also hear from Specialist Cook that Specialist Sandoval told him there was a guy in the hide-site, a child came up, was detained, and then told to go away. Sergeant Vela shot Genei Nesir Khudair Al Janabi and Specialist Sandoval was there.

Specialist Cook will also tell you that Specialist Sandoval told him they put an AK on the guy. Specialist Cook saw and will explain what he saw two to three days prior.

At the close of all the evidence you will have the answers to both questions: one, what was in the accused mind on 27 April 2007 when he murdered a man who was just cutting grass. Two, that the accused aided, abetted, and assisted in the murder of a detainee, Genei Nesir Khudair Al Janabi, from a distance of six inches with a 9mm pistol. The evidence and the answers will show that the accused is guilty of all offenses charged. Thank you.

The military judge then asked, "Does the defense have an opening statement now or do you wish to reserve?" Defense counsel replied, "We'd like to make it now, sir." We were told to proceed.

Mr. President, panel, "War is hell." General William Tecumseh Sherman said that before he burned Atlanta to the ground in the Civil War. War is hell. "The object of war is not to die for your country, but it's to make the other poor bastard die for his." George Patton, World War II.

The war in Iraq is hell, and the evidence in this case will show that the lines of this war and the battlefield of this war are blurred. The evidence will show that in this war the enemy is not always wearing an opposing uniform. The evidence will show that many of the battles of this war do not take place where one army engages another in amassed combat. The evidence will show that oftentimes the enemy of this war hides and attacks and hides again. The evidence will show that the enemy attacks and then retreats and pretends to pick up innocuous activities such as farming, repairing, or something else in an attempt to try to blend in with the community…

At the end of this trial, the evidence is going to show that on 27 April, Specialist Sandoval did shoot and kill someone. He shot the enemy. He shot the enemy who had engaged U.S. forces that morning, whom his platoon leader had authorized to shoot, and for whom his section leader had directed the shooting serving as the observer.

At the end of the day, if you have any questions in your mind that this was the enemy, you're going to hear that the body of the deceased was taken to the Iraqi Army they engaged that morning and they confirmed, "Yes, that's who engaged us." At the end of the day, the evidence is going to be very clear that Specialist Sandoval shot and killed an enemy combatant on the field of battle.

War is hell. Battle lines are sometimes unclear. What exactly happened on 11 May as far as how the individual was shot may be unclear during this case. The evidence is going to show that what is clear is that on 11 May 2007, Specialist Sandoval had nothing to do with it because he wasn't there.

And on 27 April, Specialist Sandoval was doing his job. Doing his job: go out, find people, and kill them. He was following orders. He was following the Rules of Engagement, as I said. He was following the directions of the sniper section leader.

TWELVE – CROSS-EXAMINATION

"When I have a particular case in hand, I have that motive and feel an interest in the case, feel an interest in ferreting out the questions to the bottom, love to dig up the question by the roots and hold it up and dry it before the fires of the mind."

**~ Recollected Words of Abraham Lincoln
(Stanford University Press, 1996)**

On 26 September 2007 at 1301, the court-martial was called to order.

(MILITARY JUDGE:) The court is called to order. All parties present before the court recessed are again present. The members are still absent. Trial counsel, in the last recess did the members all get a copy of a questionnaire that they can use if they have questions for witnesses?

TRIAL COUNSEL: Yes, sir, they did.

MILITARY JUDGE: Defense counsel, any objection to those?

DEFENSE COUNSEL: No objection, sir.

MILITARY JUDGE: Bailiff, call the members please.

[The bailiff did as directed, and the members entered the courtroom and were seated.] All members are now present. Trial counsel, call your first witness please.

SPECIALIST HUGO BARRAGAN

After opening statements, the prosecutors called Specialist (SPC) Hugo Barragan as their first witness. Barragan was a sniper in Sandoval's unit and was called to testify about a discussion he had with Sandoval regarding the 11 May 2007 incident. Barragan was not physically present for the incident. The prosecutors had called him because Sandoval had previously told him some bits and pieces about having detained the man and child in the hide-site and about Vela shooting the man.

The prosecutors were trying to show that Sandoval himself was somehow involved in the improper detention of the man or encouraged Vela to shoot the man. However, I had met with Barragan multiple times before trial to ask him about his testimony and on cross-examination was able to elicit the fact that Sandoval never told Barragan that he actually witnessed the detaining or shooting of the man. In fact, Barragan testified that Sandoval never said that he had anything to do with the detention or the shooting. All Sandoval actually told Barragan was a version of what *he was told* happened on 11 May 2007.

On cross-examination, Barragan testified as follows:

(Q: DEFENSE COUNSEL)

(A: SPC BARRAGAN)

Q: Specialist Barragan, when you were having this conversation with Specialist Sandoval about what happened on May 11th, Specialist Sandoval never told you that he actually saw with his own eyes the shooting, did he?

A: That's correct.

Q: And he never told you that he actually witnessed the events leading up to that shooting, correct?

A: That's correct.

Q: And Specialist Sandoval never told you that he was involved with that shooting in any way, shape, or form, correct?

A: Correct.

If the prosecutors thought they were getting their case off to a good start with some sort of admission or confession to Barragan by Sandoval, they were sorely mistaken. Their attempt completely fell flat and worked in our favor. If the jury was thinking they were going to hear some damning evidence right out of the gate, they were surely disappointed.

◆ ◆ ◆

SPECIALIST ALEXANDER FLORES

The next witness for the prosecution was Specialist (SPC) Alexander Flores. Flores testified about the 27 April 2007 mission in a way that was consistent with the testimony that had been provided at the Article 32 hearing. The problematic part of his testimony occurred when he said that before Hensley and Sandoval advanced toward the man in the field, he had witnessed the man in the field for about thirty minutes just cutting grass, leaving, and then returning to continue cutting grass.

On cross-examination however, Flores clarified that he did not know if Hensley or Sandoval had ever witnessed the man cutting grass for the long periods of time that he observed. Further, Flores outlined that the deceased individual was located very near the mortar cache site that was found later that morning by the Iraqi Army. This further supported our argument that the man was a lookout and not a farmer simply cutting grass.

Flores testified that he and Hensley walked out to catalog information and photograph the body of the deceased. Further, he testified that Sandoval was not present for the initial cataloging of the body and that at some point Hensley directed Flores to place the command wire on the body and take a picture of it. He stated that he had complied.

(Q: TRIAL COUNSEL)

(A: SPC FLORES)

Q: So you went out to the body, correct?

A: Yes.

Q: Why did you go out to the body?

A: Staff Sergeant Hensley asked if I had the camera, and I told him "Yes, I do," and he was like "Go ahead and grab it, we're going to do SSE ourselves."

Q: Now when you say SSE, you mean sensitive site exploitation, correct?

A: Yes.

Q: Which means what?

A: It means we go out to the body and we put—we take pictures and then we write down and we bag and tag whatever they had for evidence.

Q: Who went with you to the body?

A: Staff Sergeant Hensley.

Q: Did the accused go to the body with you at that time?

A: No.

Q: Why not?

A: I don't know.

Q: Did he say anything to you about it?

A: No.

Q: Did you move tactically when you went to the body?

A: No, just kind of stood up and walked over there.

Q: This is a dangerous area, correct?

A: There's a lot of civilians out there with weapons so it is kind of dangerous.

Q: But you felt it was okay to get up and walk out there?

A: Yes.

Q: What did you do when you got to the dead man?

A: Before I started taking any pictures, I turned on my camera and Staff Sergeant Hensley asked me to get my—the spool of command wire out.

Q: Where did you get the command wire?

A: While I was looking through my pack—my assault pack to get my camera out, Staff Sergeant Hensley tells somebody, "Hey, get the spool of command wire out and give it to Flores." I'm not looking; I'm just looking for my camera. By the time I looked, it's on my rucksack so I just grab it and put it in my pocket.

Q: Was it there before on your rucksack?

A: No.

Q: Had you ever seen it before?

A: No.

Q: Do you have any idea how it got there?

A: Somebody obviously put it there. I don't know who.

Q: So what did you do with the command wire?

A: After he told me to get it out, he told me to place it on the body. So, I placed the command wire on the body, took a picture, and then took different—various pictures of the body.

In his testimony, the witness for the prosecution was testifying that *he*, not Sandoval, placed the command wire on the body of the deceased.

Flores was also asked numerous questions about a conversation that he and Sandoval had about the 11 May

2007 incident. Just as with the first witness, Barragan, Flores himself was not present for the 11 May 2007 incident. Additionally, in his recollection of the conversation with Sandoval, it was unclear what Sandoval actually saw or what others told him had happened. Either way, Sandoval never admitted to Barragan that he had anything to do with the shooting or planting an AK-47 on the body.

◆ ◆ ◆

CAPTAIN MATTHEW DIDIER

Matthew Didier had been promoted from a First Lieutenant to a Captain in the time that elapsed between the shootings and the trial.

CPT Didier testified that he was the officer in charge of Sandoval and Sandoval's unit around the April and May 2007 timeframe. He further testified about specific facts of the 11 May 2007 incident, stating that there were numerous radio transmissions between himself and Hensley, who were in separate locations and that, at some point, he authorized a close kill. Didier defined a close kill as "anywhere inside the range of your long weapon that would be close to you and you would have to use something other than your rifle."

When questioned, Didier agreed that he had no knowledge of Sandoval having anything to do with placing an AK-47 on a body on 11 May 2007, or having anything to do with the 11 May 2007 shooting.

We tried to "adopt" Didier as a defense witness to immediately start asking him about the 27 April 2007 shooting, but the prosecutors objected and we were forced to wait for the defense case in order to get Didier's further input regarding the April 2007 shooting.

◆ ◆ ◆

SPECIALIST CHAD MYROM

The prosecutors next called Specialist Chad Myrom. SPC Myrom had been the photographer who reported to the area of the 11 May 2007 shooting. He was an odd witness because he had absolutely nothing to add to the case other than the fact that he had placed the body of the 11 May 2007 incident in a body-bag. The prosecutors tried to elicit additional information from Myrom, however it was clear that he did not know anything and had nothing additional to add to the case.

◆◆◆

SPECIALIST DAVID COOK

The prosecutors next called Specialist David Cook. SPC Cook testified, as had others before him, that he had a conversation with Sandoval about the 11 May 2007 "close-kill" incident. Cook, however, was not present at the 11 May 2007 incident. On cross-examination, Cook confirmed that Sandoval told him that he was pulling security during the May incident and "could not have been right there." Thus, while Sandoval had apparently told Cook a version of what had happened on 11 May 2007, we were able to explain this away by eliciting testimony that Sandoval had not actually witnessed any of the events that took place in May.

(Q: DEFENSE COUNSEL)

(A: SPC COOK)

Q: Specialist Cook, when you were having this conversation with Specialist Sandoval one to two weeks later, he never told you he was physically present right at the scene where Sergeant Vela shot the guy, correct?

A: I guess so, sir. If you're in a hide-site—I mean if he's pulling security, I don't know how far security would have pulled at that time but you could assume that he could not have been right there, sir. I don't know specifically so I can't really give you a straight answer, sir.

Q: But from what you had, based upon your conversation with Specialist Sandoval, you didn't have a reason to believe that Specialist Sandoval actually witnessed the shooting, correct?

A: Not if you're pulling security, sir.

Q: No further questions.

♦ ♦ ♦

SPECIAL AGENT CHRISTOPHER MITCHUM

The prosecutors called Special Agent Christopher Mitchum to the stand. SA Mitchum had been in the Army about seven years and was an Army CID Agent assigned to Iraq. The prosecutors called Mitchum for the purpose of establishing the name and identity of the deceased victim from the 11 May 2007 shooting. The prosecutors apparently thought that they could just put Mitchum on the stand and have him state that he talked to people and determined the name of the victim.

I began objecting on the grounds of hearsay[36]. I was essentially arguing that the only way that Mitchum learned the name of the victim was by talking with other people, thereby making his testimony hearsay and inadmissible evidence.

Getting hearsay evidence admitted at trial is a class in

---

36   Hearsay is generally defined as an out-of-court statement made by someone other than the person testifying and offered in court at the time of trial as true. The theory behind the prohibitory rule is that simply relying on someone else's word can be unreliable, and the jury should be able to hear from the person who actually made the statement so that they can be subject to critique and cross-examination.

and of itself in law school. Generally speaking you cannot put a witness on the stand and just say 'Well, I talked to this person and this is what they told me.' There are exceptions to this rule, however: the burden to state the exception to the judge is upon the lawyer trying to offer the evidence at trial. In this case, the prosecutor had apparently not considered beforehand how she was going to get this victim's name into evidence at trial and was wholly unprepared for my objections. The prosecution kept trying different questions to get the name in, and I kept objecting.

The judge let me break into the prosecutor's direct examination to ask Mitchum questions to support my objections. This is generally termed *voir diring* a witness in support of an objection. Some judges allow this and some do not. Judge Hargis had no issue with my request, and I asked Mitchum specifically if the only way he learned the name of the victim was "all by oral conversations with other individuals." Thus, I am able to clarify that everything he knew was based on inadmissible hearsay.

In the end, the judge sustained my objections and did not allow Mitchum to testify about the name of the victim of 11 May 2007. Thus, the prosecutors were now continuing the trial with a victim's name that was unknown. I considered this a huge victory because now the prosecutors were asking the jury to convict Sandoval of murdering someone whose name and identity were completely unknown. If he was just a farmer, then what was the farmer's name? I made a note to make sure that I used this fact in closing argument.

I was hoping in the back of my mind that the jurors would have a difficult time convicting Sandoval of murder when the basic question that would be asked during deliberations— "Who are we saying that Sandoval killed?"—would be met with "no idea!"

◆ ◆ ◆

SPECIAL AGENT CHRISTA SCOTT

The prosecutors next called Special Agent (SA) Christa Scott. SA Scott was the agent who had interrogated Sandoval back in Laredo, Texas, on 26 June 2007. The prosecutors had flown Scott from Texas to Iraq to testify about Sandoval's "confession." Scott had been in the Army about two years and was a relative neophyte to criminal investigations. After a few minutes of the prosecutor's questions on direct examination, I began to doubt whether Scott had ever testified before. It was clear to me that, if she had, it had been very minimal as she appeared nervous and flustered even with the guiding direct examination by the prosecutor.

SA Scott testified that she interviewed Sandoval at the Laredo Police Department after receiving a request for assistance from the Iraq CID office asking for assistance in interviewing suspects of criminal activity. Requests for assistance are commonplace in criminal investigations where one office will request that another office do something related to the case. For example, someone might be instructed to "Go interview such and such witness or go take photos of this place," or something relatively straightforward.

In theory, this makes sense to save time and resources. In practice, having an agent from another office go interview someone who is a criminal suspect is not always the best idea if the other office is not provided with the full context for the interview and all the information about the case in order to ask the right questions. This reality became apparent during Scott's testimony.

Scott testified about receiving the request for assistance and coordinating with the Laredo Police Department to go take Sandoval into custody and begin an interrogation. She talked about how she and another CID Agent approached Sandoval's house with marked units from the Laredo Police Department and said that when Sandoval came to the door and saw all the law enforcement, he remarked, "Oh, shit!"

Scott testified that law enforcement personnel handcuffed Sandoval and transported him to the police station. There, he was taken to a small room, read his "rights" on a Department of the Army Form 3881[37], advised of his right to remain silent, and informed that he was being interrogated about a "murder." Sandoval acknowledged that he understood his right to remain silent and that he would be willing to make a statement about the events of 27 April 2007.

Scott testified that during the interrogation Sandoval "admitted" certain facts to her. In actuality, the only facts Sandoval admitted to were the following: that he shot an individual on 27 April 2007 who was not "running or walking," that the individual did not demonstrate "hostile act or hostile intent" supporting the shooting, and that he placed the command wire on the deceased's body.

As for the 11 May 2007 shooting, Scott testified that she had asked very few questions about the incident. She further testified that Sandoval had stated that his only knowledge of that shooting was that he "heard that an AK-47 had been placed on an Iraqi body," but was not a witness to it and was "in a pump house at the time this incident occurred."

This was the sum and substance of Scott's testimony, and by the assured looks on the prosecutor's faces, they believed that Scott's testimony had just sealed Sandoval's fate.

On cross-examination, I outlined that two Laredo Police Department vehicles, two Laredo police officers, and three Army CID Agents rolled up on Sandoval's house on 26 June 2007 and arrested him, placed him in handcuffs, and transported him to the police station. At the station, Sandoval was placed in a small room with two-way mirrors and the interrogation began.

---

37   The Department of the Army Form 3881 (DA 3881) is a written acknowledgment by a suspect of their rights under both the U.S. Constitution and the UCMJ. They are advised of what it is believed they did wrong and their right to counsel and right to remain silent.

During cross-examination, Scott agreed that Sandoval was cooperative during the interview. She stated that she began asking him very specific questions related to his actions on 27 April 2007 and the Rules of Engagement. She then admitted, over the prosecutor's multiple objections, that she had absolutely no idea what the actual Rules of Engagement were for the area where Sandoval was operating on 27 April 2007. Scott testified that, in fact, she thought "Congress" or a "higher level" had set the Rules of Engagement for the specific area where Sandoval shot the individual on 27 April.

When I began to ask Scott detailed questions about the reasoning behind the wording of the questions she directed at Sandoval during the interrogation, she was unable to provide responses to many of the questions. She was unable to explain why she did not offer Sandoval the opportunity to hand-write his own statement—which is required by an Army regulation—and unable to provide a reason why Sandoval's statement was not videotaped or recorded in an audio form so as to capture all the specific questions and answers.

(Q: DEFENSE COUNSEL)

(A: AGENT SCOTT)

Q: You never offered to let him write his statement, correct?

A: We're not required, sir.

Q: But your CID regulation states that you are to ask them, doesn't it?

A: Yes, sir, if they would like to.

Q: And you didn't do it, did you?

A: No, sir. Our battalion policy is we will not take any handwritten statement.

Q: So your battalion policy is that you don't follow CID Regulation 195-1?

A: We added to the regulation, sir.

Q: But the regulation states that he is supposed to be able to write his statement. That's not adding is it?

A: When they say that we can—that they want them handwritten—excuse me, typed, sir, they can.

Q: So your battalion picks and chooses how it wants to follow a CID…

[Trial counsel objected based on relevance, and the military judge overruled the objection. I then resumed my questioning of SA Scott.]

Q: So your battalion picks and chooses how it wants to follow a CID regulation, correct?

A: No, sir.

Q: But it doesn't follow it, does it?

A: Yes, they do.

Q: And you didn't videotape this interrogation, did you?

A: No, sir.

Q: But you could have, couldn't you?

A: We could have, sir.

Q: And if you had videotaped it, this panel would be able to sit and watch exactly how that interrogation went down, correct?

A: Yes, sir.

Q: All the surrounding circumstances of that interrogation, correct?

A: Yes, sir.

Q: And what statements were made that weren't necessarily put in this statement, correct?

A: They would be able to hear the entire statement.

> Q: And we don't have that because you didn't do it, correct?
>
> A: We did not do it, that's right."

In addition, Scott admitted that at the time she interrogated Sandoval, she already knew from the request for assistance that Flores had admitted that it was *he* who placed "the command wire on the deceased's body on 27 April" and that she never asked Sandoval to explain that glaring discrepancy.

Additionally, Scott admitted that she had never reviewed Didier's statement as it related to how he defined the actual Rules of Engagement that were in effect for the 27 April mission. This meant that the CID Agents conducting Sandoval's interview had gotten him to "admit" that at the time of the shooting there was not a "hostile act or hostile intent" by the deceased, and yet the agents had no idea what actual Rules of Engagement were in effect. Furthermore, the agents never asked Sandoval whether he believed he was following the Rules of Engagement in place during the 27 April shooting.

◆ ◆ ◆

I had several points I intended to highlight at trial. We were in a war where the enemy operated as a chameleon, one minute appearing as an enemy combatant and the next as an unarmed civilian. When Sandoval was sent on the sniper mission on 27 April 2007, his mission was to find the enemy and kill them. That was clear. His platoon leader found the enemy, radioed the enemy's movement, and authorized Sandoval to engage and kill the enemy. Sandoval took the shot.

I intended to say in so many words, "Today, Specialist Sandoval is facing a murder charge because the Army wants to say that authorization from your platoon leader, Captain Didier, and from your sniper section leader was not enough. The Army wants to say that the shooting was not justified based on some classroom version of the Rules of Engagement where the enemy is wearing a uniform shooting at you. This war is not a classroom, and a battlefield does not afford the decision-maker the comforts of time and security."

After the close of the prosecution's case, defense attorneys are allowed to move for dismissal of charges or the entire case based on the insufficiency of the evidence as provided for under the UCMJ (as well as in civilian criminal courts). The legal standard to get a case dismissed by the military judge is very high, and motions for dismissal are almost always denied. However, we thought we had a shot at getting some of the charges dismissed and made our arguments. True to expectation, the military judge quickly denied all our requests for a dismissal and ordered us to call our first witness. Thus, we moved forward with the defense case.

THIRTEEN – THE DEFENSE CASE

"You never really understand a person until you consider things from his point of view—"

"Sir?"

"—Until you climb into his skin and walk around in it."

~ **Harper Lee, "To Kill a Mockingbird"**

SERGEANT ANTHONY MURPHY

We began our defense case by calling Sergeant Anthony Murphy as a witness. SGT Murphy was a sniper in Sandoval's unit, had known Sandoval for over two years, and been directly involved in the training of Sandoval as a sniper. Murphy was a school-trained sniper from the sniper school in Fort Benning, Georgia, and in pretrial interviews had come across as a polished, professional soldier. We thought he was the best person to lead off the defense case.

I began my questioning of Murphy by discussing sniper training in general and being a school-trained sniper, as well as his specific training of Sandoval. Murphy outlined that Sandoval had been taught in accordance with Army Field Manual 23-10 and learned the different sniper roles and responsibilities.

Murphy testified that the junior soldier is normally put in the shooter position and that the spotter is generally the senior sniper as his role is to determine the appropriate target. According to Murphy, "The spotter is the one who has so much to do. He has target identification, he has spotting, he has field-craft, he understands how to see the rounds, he knows how to adjust fire, he knows how to do everything that the shooter doesn't know how to do. The shooter just needs to know how to get into a good comfortable shooting position and exhibit the fundamentals of shooting and firing correctly."

In addition to questions related to Sandoval's training as a sniper, I also questioned Murphy regarding the specific training that was provided as to the Rules of Engagement in effect for his and Sandoval's missions. He outlined how their role was to establish positive identification of the enemy believed to be part of a mortar team and kill them.

Murphy had been present for the briefing by CPT Didier for the 27 April mission. Over many objections from the prosecutor, I was finally able to have Murphy outline the "commander's intent" for the 27 April mission. In the military, missions are briefed in the form of an operations order. An operations order describes the situation the unit faces, the mission of the unit, and what supporting activities the unit will conduct in order to achieve their commander's desired end state.

The "commander's intent" is considered the most important part of the operations order because, if all else fails and if everything gets messed up, one can achieve the mission at hand by fulfilling the commander's intent. Commander's intent might entail, for example, "take that hill" or "destroy that building." In the case of 27 April, Murphy testified that "the commander's intent was to kill or destroy the enemy mortar team."

I asked Murphy to describe the safety of the area where he and Sandoval operated on 27 April. He testified that it was classified as "Tier 1," the most dangerous area, and that, "They had mortar teams consistently bombing and targeting Iskandariyah. Shi'a militia is up there, the pressure plates, it's a bad area." Further, Murphy was able to authenticate a diagram based on his location, Didier's location, Hensley's location, and Sandoval's location on 27 April.

Murphy testified that on the morning of 27 April around 0800, he was notified via radio that CPT Didier and the Iraqi Army were taking gunfire. Didier was giving information about their locations and activities in the form of a SITREP—an acronym for "Situation Report" which is used to describe a critical situation.[38] Murphy testified that Didier outlined that his group had taken fire, and that the enemy had dropped their weapons and were fleeing in the direction of where Murphy, Hensley, Sandoval, and others were located.

Murphy witnessed Hensley and Sandoval move south in the direction of the fleeing enemy to "interdict targets" based on Didier's orders to kill the fleeing enemy. Thereafter, Murphy heard shots on the radio from the direction where Hensley and Sandoval had gone. Murphy and other snipers headed in the direction of the shots and along with Hensley located the deceased's body and began conducting sensitive site exploitation, or SSE. He described SSE as, "Basically investigate the body. Just do quick pictures of the body for evidence for intelligence, identification, and any evidence on there as the body is found."

At that point, I began asking Murphy about a ring that he saw on the finger of the deceased and whether or not he recognized the ring. I showed him some exhibits as my questions related to what Murphy was looking at in the exhibits.

(Q. DEFENSE COUNSEL)

(A. SGT MURPHY)

Q: Do you recognize that?

---

38   A SITREP, or situation report, is a briefing format used to advise friendly forces and the command of a critical situation. The report is normally provided in a specific format so that the appropriate personnel and support units in the area listening to the radio traffic can know what is going on.

A: Yes, sir.

Q: I'm going to direct you to page three of that picture.

[The witness viewed page three as directed.]

Q: Is that the person you saw on 27 April 2007?

A: Yes, sir.

Q: Was that person wearing a ring?

A: Yes, he is.

Q: Is that ring on the...

At that point mid-question, the prosecution began ferociously objecting and asking for a closed hearing. After the hearing, the Judge denied our ability to inquire further about the ring. Unfortunately, all other information about the ring was handled in a classified/sealed hearing which I cannot discuss in this book. What is clear from the unclassified transcript is that we wanted to present evidence to the jury about the ring but after the hearing with the court, we were not allowed to ask additional questions about the ring on the deceased's finger.

After the classified/sealed hearing, Murphy was recalled and testified that he had been on five to seven missions in the specific area of Abu Shemsi, Iraq, where the 27 April event occurred and had never seen men farming in the area wearing a "man-dress" like the one worn by the deceased on 27 April. Further, over the prosecution's objection, Murphy was able to state the actual Rules of Engagement that CPT Didier relayed after he had made contact with the enemy. Murphy testified that Didier stated over the radio that they were to "engage fleeing local nationals without weapons."

I asked Murphy, "So if they didn't have a weapon, you could engage?"

He replied, "Yes, sir."

♦ ♦ ♦

SERGEANT ROBERT REDFERN

We called Sergeant Redfern as a defense witness. SGT Redfern was a highly-experienced, school-trained sniper who had been on over one hundred sniper missions in Iraq. Furthermore, he had been personally involved in training Sandoval as a sniper. Redfern was present for the 11 May 2007 mission and testified that the area was dangerous and the "worst" area of operations in the entire jurisdiction of Redfern's unit. In theory, Redfern could have also been charged with criminal acts related to the 11 May 2007 incident so the Military Judge had ordered that Redfern be granted immunity for his testimony so that he could testify as a defense witness.

Redfern testified that Sandoval was present for the events of 11 May 2007 and that he had detained the individual who walked up to the hide-site. Redfern explained that the individual was detained and a poncho was placed over his head so that he could not begin recording details about the unit, their capabilities, or location. Then he and Sandoval moved out of the middle of the hide-site to an exterior location, at a pump house, to begin pulling security to see if other individuals would be approaching.

At some point, Redfern and Sandoval saw a young male be released and leave the hide-site location and thereafter two shots were heard from inside the hide-site. After detailed drawings, references to maps, and other documents, Redfern confirmed that only Hensley and Vela were present in the hide-site. Sandoval had remained on security with Redfern at the pump house; he was not present in the location where the shots were fired. Furthermore, Redfern confirmed that he never saw Sandoval with an AK-47 during the 11 May mission.

Redfern did testify that he thought there was something improper about the shooting of the detainee on 11 May, and that he discussed this with Sandoval. However, he was not *certain* of any wrongdoing and as such did not report it to the higher command. In any event, Redfern was clear that Sandoval had nothing to do with any shooting or placing an AK-47 on a body on 11 May 2007.

♦♦♦

CAPTAIN MATTHEW DIDIER
[RECALLED AS A DEFENSE WITNESS]

We recalled Captain (CPT) Didier as a defense witness to testify about the events of 27 April 2007. CPT Didier testified that he and his platoon were assigned to look for a weapons cache on the 27 April mission and that he was assigned to assist with both an Iraqi Army unit and a U.S. MiTT team who were working together to locate and destroy the enemy who were operating the cache sites.

Didier testified that he had three sniper units operating on the 27 April mission and that they had been in the area of operation for several days, looking for the enemy. Didier outlined that his teams had been briefed on the Rules of Engagement and that Sandoval had been present for all the briefings. The specific Rules of Engagement for the Iskan area of operations outlined the differences between hostile intent and hostile act.

Didier testified that on 27 April 2007, he was part of a dismounted patrol working with the Iraqi Army when they encountered enemy forces. He testified that their forces came "in contact with two individuals in dark clothing who were breaking contact north to northeast." Didier thereafter relayed this information via radio to Hensley whom he directed to "engage" the individuals if he or the members of his unit spotted them fleeing in their direction. Hensley notified Didier that he had the individuals in his sights, was observing the individuals, and was ready to take any necessary action.

Didier testified that he was told that Hensley had eyes on one of the individuals and, even though the individual was unarmed at that point, he would engage in accordance with Didier's orders because "they had broken contact and disarmed themselves not for the sole purpose of surrendering or because they're injured—they disarmed themselves to escape and then engage coalition forces in Iraq and forces again in the future."

Thereafter, Didier made it clear that given all the circumstances and taking into account the Rules of Engagement as he himself understood and implemented them in his unit, Hensley and his unit were authorized to engage. "About five or ten minutes after I had given my answer to him to engage, he informed me that he—we heard a shot, and then he informed me that they had shot and killed the individual," Didier testified, confirming that the shooting of 27 April 2007 had been entirely authorized and in fact ordered by him.

◆ ◆ ◆

SERGEANT EVAN VELA

For the next trial witness, we called Sergeant (SGT) Evan Vela. Vela was pending his own charges and did not want to testify at all. He was aware that any testimony he gave could potentially have an adverse effect on his own later trial, and his attorneys were no doubt advising him against testifying. The government originally asked the Commanding General to grant Vela immunity so that they could try to use him against Sandoval. Once granted immunity, Vela could no longer invoke his own Fifth Amendment privilege to remain silent. The Fifth Amendment protects against self-incrimination and hence criminal charges. Once immunity applies, the risk of incriminating oneself and opening oneself up to criminal charges goes away.

The prosecutors interviewed Vela in the presence of his attorneys during an evening break in the trial. They were only able to meet with Vela in the evening during the trial itself as they had to fly him to Iraq from confinement in Kuwait. Vela's attorneys (one of whom was a civilian hired by Vela's family to represent him) also had to be flown to Iraq to be there for the meeting. The way things unfolded, the government coordinated to have Vela granted immunity but decided not to call him as a witness after they'd had a chance to meet with him and review his answers to their questions before testifying at trial. Apparently, the prosecutors did not like what Vela had to say about the May incident.

After the prosecutors interviewed Vela, we interviewed him and liked what he had to say. Vela was prepared to testify to confirm that Sandoval had nothing to do with the 11 May 2007 event. At that point, we decided to call Vela as a witness for the defense in our case. Of note, we had originally objected to Vela being called as a witness by the prosecution since we were never able to interview him because, prior to being granted immunity, he had invoked his Fifth Amendment right. The military judge had ruled that he would be able to testify at the trial so long as both sides were able to interview him prior to his testimony.

Once we had decided we wanted to call Vela as a witness for the defense, there was much discussion with the military judge about the immunity issue. The government argued that immunity had only been granted for their benefit, not the benefit of the defense. The prosecutors took the extremely disappointing position that they were the only ones who could use immunity for their benefit and that only they could immunize Vela for his trial testimony. They further argued that the immunity was not "final" until they physically called him as a witness at trial. After a hearing and long argument, the judge rejected the government's arguments. As Vela had already been granted immunity, he had no choice but to testify, and he was going to testify supporting the defense's case.

Vela testified that he had served as a sniper for approximately seven months with Sandoval and had been sent to the area of Jurf as Sakhr on approximately 8 May 2007. He further testified that he and other snipers and infantry soldiers had begun prepping equipment and operations in order to start their missions on the following days. Vela testified that during the May 2007 timeframe, there was "extreme sleep deprivation, OPTEMPO[39] was very high, we had maybe a two-day break period in between three- to five-day operations."

Vela further outlined that approximately ten of the soldiers received saline IVs of liquid to keep them hydrated. This evidenced the extreme Iraq heat and fatigue ongoing during the April and May missions in the Triangle of Death. Explaining the living environment was important in that it outlined that these were combat soldiers on dangerous patrols in dangerous areas—soldiers who were also dehydrated based on the limited amount of supplies that snipers were able to carry with them on missions. Even given these facts, Vela confirmed that on the 11 May mission that Sandoval had nothing to do with placing an AK-47 or injuring anyone.

The testimony from Vela was powerful as he did not sugar-coat the interaction between himself, the local national, and Hensley. Vela testified that after the local national was in the hide-site that Hensley "went over to the local national, dropped his knee on the local national's back. He knocked the wind out of him, and the local national threw his head

---

39   OPTEMPO joins the two words "operations" and "tempo" and is a term used to describe the tempo or moving pace of military operations.

back, and Staff Sergeant Hensley grabbed him by the mouth and told him to shut up or he was going to kill him."

Vela testified that "Staff Sergeant Hensley then positioned the local national. He unbound his hands and so I thought we were going to let him go; at this point we had already let the boy go. He asked me if I was ready, and I just thought that he was asking me if I was pulling security, which I was. I had the pistol up, and he had quickly moved out of the way, and I heard the word "shoot," and I don't remember pulling the trigger and didn't hear the gun fire. I just came through and the guy was dead, and it took me a second to realize that the shot had come from the pistol and it was in my hand."

I asked, "When this occurred where was Specialist Sandoval?"

Vela replied, "He was in the pump house."

♦ ♦ ♦

SERGEANT FIRST CLASS TARROL PETERSON

Prior to trial, the MG Lynch had disapproved our request to bring in a sniper expert to explain certain sniper concepts and regulations to the military panel. Given that this was denied, we were ultimately forced to present the issue and request to the military judge. The judge had the authority to essentially overrule the Commanding General and require that the prosecutors produce necessary witnesses to a court-martial. The judge saw how this would be very important and helpful to the military panel and granted our request for a sniper expert, ordering the prosecutors to fly our requested expert to Iraq from Fort Benning, Georgia, home of the U.S. Army Sniper School.

We were able to get Sergeant First Class Tarrol Peterson,

the enlisted "officer in charge" of the U.S. Army Sniper School at Fort Benning, Georgia, appointed as an expert witness in sniper training and tactics. SFC Peterson had graduated from the Army Infantry School, Sniper School, Airborne School, Air Assault School, Rappel Master School, and a number of other different schools and courses related to small unit infantry operations. Furthermore, Peterson had previously been specifically requested by the Vice Chief of Staff of the Army for a special assignment as a sniper in Iraq. The details of this "special assignment" remain classified.

Peterson was the venerable real deal and had deployed more than three times, including combat operations in Somalia, Haiti, and Iraq: these were the unclassified missions that he was able to talk about. He had also written or edited many of the Army's regulations and policies regarding deploying snipers in combat. When it came to sniper operations, there was no one more experienced or trusted than Peterson. His resume also included advising the leadership of the other military branches on sniper operations as he had been recently selected to serve on a board for the Marine Corps to rewrite its own sniper manuals.

We were able to have Peterson present for the entire trial so that he could give his opinions from an expert perspective about both Sandoval's actions and that of his unit. Peterson testified as to the implementation of Army Field Manual 23-10 ("Sniper Training") in actual combat operations. As an expert, he was able to give expert analysis and opinions, and we felt that this would be helpful to the jury as none of the panel members had ever served as a sniper.

When I was first detailed the case, I had reached out to instructors from the Army Sniper School to discuss the case. I learned that my reading of the sniper regulation was not totally off base. The spotter is responsible for the target and the Rules of Engagement; the shooter is not. Sandoval was the shooter, not the spotter.

(Q: DEFENSE COUNSEL)

(A: SFC PETERSON)

Q: The regulation states that a sniper must be able to calmly and deliberately kill targets that may not pose an immediate threat to him. What does that mean?

A: Roger, sir. What that means is that the person or individual or whatever you are going to shoot may not pose a threat to you. If someone or a vehicle—I shoot vehicles at 1800 meters; that's over a mile. That vehicle usually is not a threat to me. It could be a threat to somebody else, or that person 1800 meters could be a threat to someone at a half mile away. It could be a threat to someone and I get the kill, that target gets hit.

Q: Is that same principle taught at the sniper school to Army snipers?

A: Roger that, sir...

In other words, Peterson was saying that he himself, a highly-respected sniper and an expert in his field, had shot at targets so far away from him, they could not possibly have been perceived as direct threats to him. Furthermore, he explained that posing a threat to others was sufficient basis for the kills.

I resumed my questioning of Peterson as follows:

Q: And the regulation says that it's much easier to kill in self-defense or in the defense of others than it is to kill without apparent provocation. The sniper must not be susceptible to emotions such as anxiety or remorse. What does that mean?

A: Roger, sir. That means—this section of the manual is for selection for someone to be a sniper. I think later it's going to go on to talk about if someone is looking to be a cowboy or looking for—just looking to be a sniper because it sounds cool—then that's not the person you want. You want a person who can do the job and be able to do it without having to think about it or question should I do this and am I doing the right thing? They have to know they're doing the right thing and have to be able to pull the trigger, and it's not an easy thing to do. Where it's talking about in self-defense, it's a lot easier to shoot someone who's running at you with an AK at 100 meters than it is to shoot somebody who is walking around with an AK who has no idea that you're there because you're in a covered and concealed position from a half mile away. That person has no idea that they're about to get shot. It's a lot harder to do that than to shoot someone who is right in your face. That's what that is talking about, sir.

Related to Sandoval's actions on 27 April 2007, we wanted to make it clear that even if there were questions about the kill or the appropriate target, any fault was on Hensley and not Sandoval. Peterson explained this in very simple and precise terms to the jury as I continued my examination of him.

Q: When Field Manual 23-10 says the observer is to select an appropriate target, what training at Fort Benning in the sniper school, and training of snipers in theater—how does that concept relate to the Rules of Engagement?

A: Roger, sir. At Fort Benning, from the day they get there, we have them identify a sniper buddy. A sniper buddy is always going to be within arm's reach of them. When that person is out on the range, he's the one who says, "Okay, this is what your target is," and he calls out the target. Say he wanted to shoot target A; target A is 790 meters and he calls out target A. The sniper says, "Yes, I see target A," so he identifies it in the scope. The spotter is the one who told him which one the target was, and then the sniper then tells the spotter how far away it is. At that time, the spotter gives him the data for his gun. The sniper then puts it on the gun and tells the spotter, "Yes, I am ready to fire," or whatever dialog they have developed. Most of the time it's, "Snipers up," and then the spotter then tells him to send it. When he tells him to send it, he fires that rifle within a second to a second in a half. No more time than that because that bullet must go out the rifle and get downrange before the wind changes—anything changes; that bullet has to get downrange because that spotter has figured out, "Okay, the wind is perfect right now and I want you to fire right now." When he says, "Send it," that sniper's job is to send that bullet right now, not to think about it or go, "Oh well. I think maybe I…" because he can't see the wind like the spotter sees it. The spotter has different optics and has more experience as a key to be able to do that job.

Q: Who is the senior person in a sniper section?

A: The senior person in the sniper section is usually the sniper squad leader or sniper section sergeant.

At this point, we believed that Peterson had cemented our defense for the 27 April shooting, and he had explained that Sandoval's actions in pulling security on the hide-site on 11 May 2007 were also proper. While pulling security on the hide-site, Sandoval would have been focused to look for individuals or units approaching the hide-site and not focused on what was happening in the hide-site. As such, it was entirely plausible that Sandoval had no idea what was going on with the 11 May shooting as he was properly pulling security.

After many objections by the prosecutors and rephrasing,

I was finally able to elicit the following very precise answers from Peterson as it directly related to Sandoval's actions. My first set of questions related to the 11 May 2007 incident, as follows:

Q: Sergeant First Class Peterson, are you able to make an expert determination as to whether Specialist Sandoval's actions on May 11th by moving out to the pump house were in compliance with Army sniper training?

A: By moving out to the pump house, sir, reestablishing security, that was what you're supposed to do. Any of my soldiers—the first thing they would have done if we had gotten compromised would be to regain security. It's the first thing you do always.

Q: And what would have been, under Army sniper training and sniper tactics, his responsibilities in the pump house?

A: To provide security. That's his basic soldier task right there. If someone tells you to provide security or no one tells you to provide security, that's one of those discipline things that—okay, we're compromised and I need to move somewhere and secure an area...

Then I switched gears and began to ask about the 27 April incident.

Q: Sergeant First Class Peterson, Specialist Sandoval's actions on 27 April, in taking a shot, at the direction of his sniper section leader, is that within—is that following Army sniper training and Army sniper tactics?

A: Roger that, sir. He followed his sniper section sergeant who trained him, told him to take the shot, so he took the shot. There was no hesitation and like I said before, you're trained that when a spotter tells you to shoot, you shoot.

◆ ◆ ◆

SERGEANT EVAN VELA

After we rested the defense case, the prosecutors recalled Sergeant Evan Vela as a witness. At first, we were not sure why they wanted to put Vela back on the stand. As their direct examination began, however, it became clear that they were trying to impeach him from a statement he gave CID in June 2007 about Sandoval's location on 11 May 2007. Vela was adamant that his June 2007 statement was not what he actually said; however, the testimony was best described as a ramble of thoughts and unclear facts.

On cross-examination, we were able to clarify the confusion by pointing out that Vela had met with CID on two separate occasions, the first for seven hours and the second for two hours. Clearly, all of what was discussed was not encapsulated in either sworn statement. In light of the fact that CID does not audiotape or videotape their interrogations/ interviews, we were hoping that the jury would agree that if there were doubts or speculation about what Vela actually said, they would not hold anything against Sandoval.

The prosecutors then tried to admit Vela's entire written statement into the record. We strenuously objected, and the military judge agreed that it was hearsay and inadmissible.[40]

There was no follow-up. Hence, that's how the prosecutors chose to rest their case—by trying to admit improper evidence to the jury and getting denied by the military judge. We rested for the evening and began to prepare for our closing argument.

---

40   Notably, at trial, Vela could have been asked to testify about his prior statement or been cross-examined about it, but just trying to introduce the entire previous statement itself was hearsay and inadmissible.

FOURTEEN - CLOSING ARGUMENTS

"It is not what a lawyer tells me I may do, but what humanity, reason, and justice tell me I ought to do."

~ Edmund Burke, Second Speech on Conciliation, 1775

The prosecutors led the close of their case with a rambling, and in my opinion, an incoherent and neophytical closing statement.

I asked you when this case began to think about two things: one, what was in the accused's mind on 27 April 2007 when he raised his sniper rifle and he shot the man he saw in that field; and two, on 11 May 2007, where was the accused? Focus on those two things and it will be clear that what happened on 27 April 2007 was murder and what happened on 11 May 2007 was also murder by the accused.

It is important in terms of 27 April 2007 to understand the timeline. To understand the accused's mind when he lifted his sniper rifle and shot that man, you have to know what was going on in his head. Look at the facts according to the accused. Specialist Flores, Staff Sergeant Hensley, the accused, Sergeant Murphy are in the hide-site: a dry canal in Abu Shemsi, Iraq. Flores told you that he saw a man cutting grass and then the man left and then Flores fell asleep. The accused said that he saw a man walk up a while later and "pop a squat." Look at his sworn statement as you deliberate and understand that is exactly what the accused saw. The accused also, in his statement, said that he saw no hostile act, no hostile intent on the part of this individual who walked up and "popped a squat." Flores also told you that he saw the man again, around the same time as the accused, squatting, only he was cutting grass. He had a sickle which you will see in the pictures, which you will also have as you deliberate.

They watched that man for ten minutes and then they decided to flank. Staff Sergeant Hensley and the accused flank this individual. As they are flanking this individual, they are not walking tactically. In fact, they are seen according to Specialist Flores. The man looks up and sees them and goes back to cutting grass. The accused and Staff Sergeant Hensley are in the tree line for another five to ten minutes and then the accused shoots this man. In that timeline, there is no hostile act, there is no hostile intent shown on the part of this individual to the eyes of Specialist Sandoval.

At the time he pulled the trigger, he didn't know if this man was anybody other than just some man out there cutting grass. It's a farming community. You heard testimony that it's a farming community, that it's a regularly conducted activity. And there were people out there during that entire mission. One day this man is out there cutting grass, and the next minute he's dead.

The most important thing about the timeline is after. In the time after the kill when Specialist Sandoval, the accused, walks out to the body—that's not something they normally do, not something snipers normally do, you heard that testimony from the expert. Yet they walk out to the body, they expose themselves, and then they come back to the hide-site.

The wire in this case is the biggest clue to what is going on in the accused's mind on 27 April 2007. Why would he, as he admits in his sworn statement, plant wire if he thought that was a good kill? Why would anyone? And then he didn't want to go back out to the body. Everybody else went out to the body, but he didn't want to go. He admits to placing the wire. He had to justify his kill, because he knew it was not a good kill. He admits that the ROE requires hostile act, hostile intent. And all he saw this man do was walk up and "pop a squat."

Let's turn to 11 May: what matters is where Specialist Sandoval was on 11 May 2007. When the man walks up to the hide-site, when that person walks up to the hide-site, it's the accused who takes charge. It's the accused who has his 9mm in his holster; who gives that holster to Sergeant Vela and says, "Train it on him." It is the accused who detained this individual.

As he told Specialist Barragan and Specialist Flores, he doesn't mention an AK to them. The victim is detained; there is no AK-47. The victim is searched; there's still no AK-47. And what is the accused doing this whole time? He is providing security for that search and then he's providing security in that hide-site. That little boy walks in; there is some discrepancy when you heard from the defense witnesses; there's some issues as far as where he was at what specific time. But the most important thing about those witnesses' testimony is that none of them testified exactly the same way.

None of them said the accused was here at this specific time; yes, the accused was there at this specific time. Some of them said he was in the pump house before the little boy came in, some of them said afterward. Some of them said that he—that communication was made between folks in the pump house and folks in the hide-site during this whole time; and the people in the pump house, Sergeant Redfern, said that it didn't happen. Sergeant Redfern tells you that he has no clue what happened, because he's in the pump house the whole time.

Again, go back to what the accused told Specialist Barragan and Specialist Flores shortly after this actually occurred; the most recent conversations we have, in time in comparison to when this occurred, is with Specialist Barragan, Specialist Flores, and Specialist Cook. "This one isn't going anywhere." The accused told both Specialist

Barragan and Specialist Flores the same thing—that Staff Sergeant Hensley was with Sergeant Vela (as Sergeant Vela testified) and Henley asked Vela, "Are you ready?" Sergeant Vela took a long pause and then he shot the victim twice in the head.

The accused told both Specialist Barragan and Specialist Flores exactly what happened in that hide-site that day. And there's still no AK-47 on this man! Until Staff Sergeant Hensley takes it out of his pack and puts it on the victim. Sandoval knows this too. He tells Specialist Cook, "They put an AK-47," and he admits in that statement that he knows that an AK-47 was planted on the victim.

Premeditation is an element to this 11 May murder. Pay attention to what the accused says and where he was. There is that long pause before Sergeant Vela pulls the trigger. A pause that Sandoval describes to both Specialist Barragan and Specialist Flores.

Let's briefly touch on the humane treatment issue. The accused knew it was wrong for Staff Sergeant Hensley to kick that detainee; and that—for Staff Sergeant Hensley, Sergeant Vela, and everyone in that hide-site to assist in the murder of that detainee. He knew that he was supposed to treat detainees humanely; to ensure the humane treatment; to protect them.

The accused was on guard when this man walked up. He saw the searches. He knew this man walked in unarmed and unmolested by anybody in that hide-site. That that man cooperated in every way with all five soldiers in that hide-site. At the very least, he stood idly by while that man, that innocent man, was summarily executed by those soldiers in that hide-site.

Sergeant Vela told you Staff Sergeant Hensley kicked the detainee square in the back; knocked his breath out. At the most, he participated in this murder. He owed a duty to that detainee, and he failed in ensuring the humane treatment of that detainee.

Again, I ask you, pay attention to what was in the accused's mind on 27 April 2007 and where the accused was on 11 May 2007. He knew he had no justification; no authorization to murder that man on 27 April 2007 who was only cutting grass. He had no justification so he had to create it; he had to plant wire. And on 11 May 2007, the accused was in that hide-site. He helped detain that man and he helped search that man; he gave Sergeant Vela his weapon; and then in the end, he helped murder him. And then he planted an AK-47 on his remains, just like the wire, to cover it up.

The government has proven the elements of all offenses charged and shown beyond a reasonable doubt that the accused, Specialist Jorge Sandoval, Jr., committed the unpremeditated murder of an unknown deceased on 27 April 2007, wrongfully placed command wire on his remains. And on 11 May 2007, committed the premeditated murder of an unknown person, failed to ensure humane treatment for a detainee, and wrongfully placed an AK-47 on that person's remains.

The government respectfully requests that you find the accused guilty of all offenses charged.

There was more emotion than substance, and the argument was such a ramble that I did not believe it would be productive to make specific responses to the allegations. I sat in my chair, ready to pounce the entire time and, after what seemed like an eternity, it was my turn at the closing argument.

We discussed in my opening statement that "war is hell." General Sherman said it in the Civil War. Other generals have said it. Politicians have said it. "War is hell" and people die. A soldier's job oftentimes is to shoot people, is to kill the enemy—that's a soldier's job.

On 27 April this soldier, Specialist Sandoval, had a job, and you heard from a number of witnesses about what that job was. The job was to go out, as a U.S. Army sniper, on a sniper mission, in one of the most dangerous areas of Iraq, and find individuals emplacing mortars or having anything to do with mortars, and kill them—take them out.

On that day he wasn't alone, he was with his sniper team, he was with members of the coalition forces, he was with members of the Iraqi Army, all of them in the Abu Shemsi area. His spotter that day, his observer, was the sniper section leader—an NCO—a non-commissioned officer superior to this specialist. That is his observer. That is his spotter.

They go out on this mission and on the third day the platoon leader, the person who sets the Rules of Engagement for this soldier's missions, who briefs the missions, who briefs the Rules of Engagement, who sets the standard, comes on the radio and says, "The enemy is fleeing in your direction. Insurgents have attacked us. I'm with the Iraqi Army. We've been attacked in this location. They're fleeing in your direction and they're wearing this black clothing. Engage."

Staff Sergeant Hensley, the non-commissioned officer, comes back on the radio once he spots the insurgents and says, "I have eyes on." Staff Sergeant Hensley regained PID [positive ID]. And he regained PID based on what the platoon leader told him these individuals looked like, and the platoon leader said where these individuals came from. Staff Sergeant Hensley said this one individual has started cutting grass. Popped a squat and started cutting grass.

You heard from Captain Didier's own mouth, he authorized them to engage. The platoon leader authorized it. Staff Sergeant Hensley directed it to Specialist Sandoval. Specialist Sandoval did his duty. One shot, one kill. He dropped him.

Was Specialist Sandoval supposed to have had a big picture of what was going on, on 27 April? Was he really? Was Specialist Sandoval supposed to have known that the order was lawful or unlawful? Is that really the standard by which a Specialist in the United States Army should be judged? Was this Specialist supposed to know whether Captain Didier's order about the Rules of Engagement, was lawful or unlawful? Was he supposed to have known the specific details of what happened in the Iraqi Army engagement? Was he supposed to have known whether what Staff Sergeant Hensley was telling him was lawful or unlawful?

After all, Staff Sergeant Hensley wasn't just a Staff Sergeant, wasn't just a superior non-commissioned officer, wasn't just the sniper section leader: he was also in the position to be providing that guidance as far as to shoot or not to shoot. And there's an Army Field Manual, which you have into evidence, which very clearly explains this. Specialist Sandoval is supposed to rely upon what Staff Sergeant Hensley tells him. That's his job—you rely upon what your observer tells you to do.

Was Specialist Sandoval supposed to know to question that? When he's down in the reeds of two- to three-foot-high grass, looking through the scope of his rifle, looking only at a man's head? Was he supposed to know to question all of that? When he's in the middle of a battlefield, in one of the most dangerous areas of Iraq, an area where the enemy does not wear a uniform. Is that what is expected of Specialist Sandoval?

No. Absolutely not. There no way that Specialist Sandoval was supposed to be able to judge that order was unlawful. Absolutely no way.

If he had questioned that order, if he decided, "Let's go ahead and question that order," what is he questioning? He is questioning what his platoon leader has just relayed about an engagement for which he is not privy to the details, nor was he at. So he could be questioning the situation report based on a situation where he doesn't know what happened. To do that he is going to be questioning his superior non-commissioned officer; he is going to be questioning his sniper section leader; and he's going to be questioning his observer. And he's going to be doing all of this in about one second, as he's down in the reeds on a battlefield in Iraq looking through a scope at an enemy. Is he supposed to do that? No, he is not. It's not what is expected of a soldier in the United States Army.

You heard an analogy, a hypothetical about shooting a little girl.[41] We all heard that analogy; I think it was brought up twice. About, well, if the direction was to shoot a little girl, isn't he not supposed to do it? Shouldn't he know not to shoot the little girl? Doesn't he have a duty not to shoot the little girl?

Well, back in the States, walking down a street in Chicago—maybe. On a field training exercise—maybe. But in Abu Shemsi, Iraq, on 27 April, where the enemy has just attacked Iraqi forces and U.S. forces and where his platoon leader has come on the radio describing this attack and describing where the attackers are fleeing; and describing the outfit which the fleeing attackers are wearing; and then an individual goes into a field and pretends to cut grass who is not wearing a farming outfit.?

[The defense counsel retrieved Defense Exhibit A and Prosecution Exhibit 7 from the court reporter.] I'm showing you Prosecution Exhibit 7: does that look like a farming

---

41   The prosecution had used an analogy earlier in the case during the cross-examination of two defense witnesses whether it is proper to for a sniper shooter to shoot a little girl in a pink dress who was walking to school if the sniper spotter says to shoot the girl. The analogy was ridiculous and not applicable to the facts of Sandoval's case, or to a battlefield.

outfit? Does that look like this individual is ready to go to the fields? No. Because he wasn't. He wasn't a farmer: he was the insurgent who had just attacked U.S. forces, and he's there in that field hiding and possibly gathering surveillance on where these snipers are.

Specialist Flores said a lot of very interesting things. He claims that this insurgent had eyes on. Eyes on? He has eyes on their movement? And you're saying we can't take this individual out? Come on. Specialist Sandoval thought this was the enemy. Specialist Sandoval was given an instruction to fire; he had no reason to question it.

At the end of the day, it's also clear, when you look at the big picture of what happened, this individual was an enemy combatant. An enemy combatant. He had attacked U.S. troops, he had fled, he was taken out, and he was also identified by the Iraqi Army.

Do not set aside testimony that you heard read from Captain Mulvaney. This individual was taken to the Iraqi Army and the Iraqi Army said, "Yes, that is who attacked us." And who is this person? The government has not produced a name. They've charged a United States soldier with "murder of an unknown deceased." And they've asked you to convict him of "murder of an unknown deceased?"

Come on. If this person was a farmer, don't you think they could go figure it out? Couldn't they go around in that community and knock on a few doors and say, "Hey, are you missing a farmer? Did your farmer not come back from the fields today? And what is his name?"

They haven't produced a death certificate; they haven't produced an identification card; they have produced nothing. But they want you to convict a soldier for murdering this person.

Not today! Not in a war. Not when it is a Specialist in the United States Army who received guidance from his platoon leader and then a directive from his sniper section leader, his Staff Sergeant. Not today.

You heard about a statement that Specialist Sandoval made on 26 June 2007; you saw Special Agent Scott come here and talk about that statement; and you heard how a little convoy of vehicles rolled up in front of Specialist Sandoval's house while he was on leave. Five members of law enforcement—it's like a version of *Cops*—it's surprising that they didn't bang the door down. Five members of law enforcement roll up at Specialist Sandoval's house, take him outside, handcuff him, take him to the police station, put him in a room with two-way mirrors, and put two CID Agents in there with a laptop. They're there to get something. They're there to get a confession!

Now they have their request for assistance. You heard from Agent Scott, they know what they're there to do, and they do get Specialist Sandoval to admit some things. They get him to admit about not having hostile intent or hostile act. But what's really important about that statement [are] two things. One, Special Agent Scott had the statement from Specialist Flores. She was already aware Specialist Flores had fully confessed to planting this wire and taking pictures of it.

Agent Scott, why not ask Specialist Sandoval to explain? Why not confront him with this apparent inconsistency? Why not? Maybe it's because she didn't want to hear the answer. Maybe the answer didn't help her case.

Now, you also heard that in that statement he said about the Rules of Engagement, "No hostile act." But what they didn't have was Captain Didier's statement. And you heard them, they did not have any statement from Captain Didier. It might have been important to know if the platoon leader had communicated that he had hostile act; it might have been important to know if the platoon leader had communicated that, "You are good to engage." It might have been important to know that the section leader gave an order to engage.

That sworn statement, gathered without knowing Didier's statement, is like gathering a statement from somebody who broke into a house—you've got some individual who broke into a house—who broke down the door, and he runs into that house and he goes and grabs a woman out of bed, and throws her over his shoulder and runs outside, and you question this person to get him on breaking and entering, assault, possible kidnapping. You're asking him all of these questions, but wouldn't it be important to know that that person was a firefighter? Wouldn't that be an important fact, to know why this person did all of these things? Wouldn't it be important to know that this soldier is a sniper and that the sniper section leader authorized it? If the scout platoon leader directed it, wouldn't that be important? Yes.

But they didn't know that and they didn't ask Specialist Sandoval about it. That statement shouldn't be taken with a grain of salt; you need to take the whole salt shaker when you look at that statement, because even with those facts you heard that they didn't even gather it in accordance with their own regulation, their own procedure. They didn't follow a number of them; they're supposed to let him write his statement, his words. She typed it. You heard that.

She wanted to call it a friendly interview, as if it was a job application. That's not an interview when you have two vehicles rolling up to your house; five agents, three CID Agents, and two Laredo police officers, coming out; being pulled off of leave after serving over in Iraq; thrown in a room with two agents and double-way mirrors: it wasn't an interview. And you heard her say after being questioned about it, their own regulation says that's an interrogation. And that's what happened. They got what they wanted out of that statement and you all should look at that statement in that light. Take it with the whole salt shaker.

You heard from Specialist Flores he planted the wire; you

heard that in this court, from his own mouth, on this stand. He planted the wire. He told you when he did it, he described the wire, he told you that he had put it in a pocket. He said he took it out of the pocket, he placed it on the chest, and he took pictures of it. Exactly what you've got in Prosecution Exhibit 7 [the defense counsel held up Prosecution Exhibit 7 for the panel to view].

You've got the pocket, [the defense counsel then flipped to the next photograph in Prosecution Exhibit 7] you've got the chest. Just like Specialist Flores said he did.

11 May 2007: let's get this straight, make sure that we're clear. A soldier has been charged with murder, been brought to trial for murdering someone, for which the person who actually pulled the trigger came into the courtroom, Sergeant Vela, and said he did it "Yes, I shot the guy." Specialist Sandoval had nothing to do with it. Specialist Sandoval was in the pump house.

The prosecutor tried to elicit a prior inconsistent statement: "Well, you didn't always say that." You heard Sergeant Vela, "Yes, I did. I drew maps." In those maps, where was Specialist Sandoval? "He was in the pump house." You heard from Sergeant Redfern: take his testimony for what you may, take his demeanor for what you may, but one thing is certain about what he said and what he always said—Specialist Sandoval was in the pump house.

The government would have you believe there was some big enterprise going on that day. But the truth is, this soldier was doing his job. Somebody had walked up on their hide-site—again, in one of the most dangerous areas of Iraq—and they don't know who he is. They detain him. Isn't that what you're supposed to do? Isn't that the five S's? Search, segregate—aren't there the five S's? I wrote them down because I couldn't remember them. [The defense counsel retrieved his notes from the defense table.] Search, silence, segregate, speed, and safeguard. Isn't that what's taught?

Search, silence, segregate, speed, and safeguard? Isn't that what they did? The guy's talking, we've got to get this guy silent. He may bring other insurgents in the area. Isn't that what they did?

And then wasn't Specialist Sandoval placed on security? And isn't that what snipers do? Didn't you hear from Sergeant First Class Peterson, "That's not what only snipers do, it's what soldiers do?" Get perimeter security; get sectors of fire set up; we don't know what's going on.

And during that time Sergeant Vela shot the guy. That's a problem. And that may be a crime. Sergeant Vela's not on trial here; Specialist Sandoval is. And they've charged him with murder. Because he was in the area and because they passed the one 9mm that they have, so that security could be pulled with a 9mm; and then when this was all said and done, the 9mm went back to Specialist Sandoval because he was carrying the holster.

So he's somehow involved in this murder? What? What did he do? How did he aid or abet or incite or anything with this murder? Nothing. He probably should have reported it, but that's not what he's on trial for. He's on trial for murdering this individual.

And the AK-47? Who came in here and said Specialist Sandoval had something to do with it? Who testified that they ever saw Specialist Sandoval with an AK-47? Who testified that they ever saw Specialist Sandoval handed an AK-47 from somebody and walk to the body and place it on it? Who said it? No one. Zero.

The government has charged this soldier with a crime, brought him to trial, and shown you zero evidence that he did it. Should he be convicted? Is that the standard really? Zero evidence? Is the standard that we're going to convict a soldier of murder for going on a sniper mission and following orders? Following orders which he thought were lawful?

Following orders of killing an enemy combatant for which it was justified? Planting evidence, because CID got him to say a few words when they're trying to get a confession out of their interrogation? A statement which doesn't make sense; a statement which doesn't make sense when they never talked about Specialist Flores's statement with him; a statement that doesn't make sense when taken in the context that they had no idea what Didier had said or done, and they never asked Specialist Sandoval about it.

And then on 11 May a murder for which he wasn't even at? Inhumane treatment which wasn't? Silencing somebody is not against anything. The government pulled some regs, but you heard from Captain Didier, they never train on those regs. They acted reasonably out there, reasonably detained people, and that's what happened. Somebody got killed, yes, but Sergeant Vela did it, not Specialist Sandoval.

AK-47? Where that's from? You be the judge. Where that charge came from and what evidence they presented, you be the judge of that.

"War is hell." People die; people get killed. We are in a battlefield; we are fighting an enemy today that's unclear, and the battle-line is blurred in cities, towns, fields. The government is saying that Specialist Sandoval should have figured it all out right there on that field in about three seconds. He should have figured it all out and had all the answers? No. That's not what is expected of a soldier. This soldier is guilty of nothing. He was at the wrong place on 11 May. He was unfortunately on a mission when Sergeant Vela shot a guy in the head, but he didn't have anything to do with it.

Now on 27 April, this soldier was doing his job. Send him home; let him go. The truth will set him free, and you have heard the truth. You heard the truth from Captain Didier, you heard it from Sergeant Vela: you've heard the truth. And the truth is what happened.

We ask for a finding of not guilty for all charges. Let this soldier go—he didn't do anything wrong.

♦ ♦ ♦

Military Judge: Trial counsel, do you have a rebuttal argument?

Trial Counsel: Yes, sir.

Military Judge: You may proceed.

Trial Counsel: Thank you, sir. Your Honor, members of the panel, I just want to touch on a few things: One, you heard a lot of testimony about the ROE; what is the ROE? What was in the accused's mind on 27 April 2007, when he shot that man; when he murdered that man? He knows that what he needs is to see a hostile act or hostile intent.

The other issue is did PID survive? Was there PID and did it survive? What do we have?

We have testimony that there may or may not have been a firefight; we have testimony that that may have been communicated to Captain Didier; we have testimony that he passed it along to the folks in that hide-site, to Staff Sergeant Hensley and the accused. In fact, that is in the accused's statement, that he did—there is—there's some communication. Some communication; not specified from Captain Didier.

But what did we also hear?

We also heard that the ROE is communicated at the beginning of every single mission. So if the ROE changes— the ROE suddenly changes—a soldier, a reasonable soldier, a reasonable person, which is the standard required, would have known that any order or authorization based on that change was an illegal order; was not lawful.

And then, I want to bring you back, bring you back to that timeline; the timeline we talked about. Think of the amount of time it took, if this individual was the same person, for him to get all the way over to where the snipers were. Think about what was communicated, that very, very general description. Think about the fact that any identification, the identification spoken about in that stipulation, that witness would have testified that an identification was made; that an identification was made when the individual's head was covered? The victim's head was covered; all he could see was the clothing; all he could see was a person wearing dark clothing. And what do we know?

Again, what does the accused know about what happened on 27 April? He sees an individual wearing dark clothing, walk up not run. But the known individuals were running, wearing dark clothing, in the same general direction.

What was the authorization?

"If you have PID, you can engage."

If they don't have PID, they can't engage. Look at that description; look at the length of time. This is not a decision that was made in three seconds. Those soldiers watched this man, from their hide-site, for a period of time, for ten minutes; decided to leave their hide-site, walk down the canal; waited another five to ten minutes, continued to watch this individual; and then they took him out. He was murdered.

Flores didn't confess. All Flores told you is that he did exactly what Specialist Myrom said. He was told to put wire on the body in order to take pictures. To document evidence that he believed was already on the body. He did not..."

Defense Counsel: I object, Your Honor.

Military Judge: Basis?"

Defense Counsel: She's arguing facts not in evidence."

Military Judge: Which fact are you talking about?"

Defense Counsel: He believed there was already wire on the body. I don't think Specialist Flores said he believed there was already wire on the body.

Military Judge: All right, sustained. Members of the court, you heard all of the evidence and when you go back into the deliberation room, just rely on the evidence as you remember hearing it. As I stated earlier, arguments of counsel are not evidence. You may proceed.

Trial Counsel: Thank you, sir.

Flores didn't confess, he conducted a necessary function. He conducted sensitive site exploitation as Specialist Myrom did. Which involves, as Specialist Myrom testified, moving objects around as directed. Specialist Flores is also not on trial here, the accused is.

CID didn't coerce that statement. You heard Special Agent Scott testify that that interview was actually one of the easiest ones she had ever done. He was extremely cooperative. It only took two hours. He wasn't handcuffed until he got to the vehicle. He was offered breaks. And then they took him to dinner. He signed his statement; he initialed this statement [the trial counsel held up Prosecution Exhibit 4 to the panel]; and he dated this statement in front of two agents following their battalion policy. He wasn't dragged out of the house, he was read his rights. He understood those rights, and he signed that document stating that he knew and understood his rights. And he knew what they wanted to talk to him about. They even took him to dinner.

Let's talk about Redfern's alibi, the pump house. How do we know that that is not true? We know it because it was part of the original cover story that Redfern, Sandoval, and Sergeant Hand were in the pump house. We know from Sergeant Vela's testimony that Sergeant Hand was actually out on that berm that whole time. Sergeant Hand was never in the pump house. And then you hear one story from Sergeant Vela, and another story from Sergeant Redfern, as far as who was where and when and doing what.

At the end of the day, Sergeant Redfern has every reason to need to stick to that alibi. He admits that almost every single other part of his original story is false, except the pump house. The pump house keeps him out of trouble. It's also not true because of what you heard from Specialist Barragan, Specialist Flores, and Specialist Cook.

Again, the accused talked to them, he spoke to them, he confided in his friends, shortly after 11 May 2007, and described line by line what went on in that hide-site. He describes the little boy who came into the hide-site. The little boy who cried, "Father, father." He talks about detaining the individual. He talks about the look on Sergeant Vela's face after the murder. Most of all he never mentions the pump house, not to Specialist Cook, Specialist Barragan, or Specialist Flores. He never mentions the pump house. And he also had those conversations with Sergeant Redfern between the time that he confided in Specialist Barragan, Specialist Flores, and Specialist Cook; and the time he talked to CID. That's where the alibi is. That's where that story comes from; it comes from Sergeant Redfern.

Again, I touched a little bit on it—I'm going to go over it again: Sergeant Vela and Sergeant Redfern don't remember exactly where the accused was on 11 May 2007. They can't remember who had the 9mm first; they can't remember— Sergeant Redfern can't remember if he was on the left or the right of the accused; if the accused was on his left or his right in that pump house. And then there's Sergeant Redfern's story about two guys that may have been in the hide-site that day? No one else, to include Sergeant Vela, ever mentioned anything about two individuals in the hide-site.

Sergeant Vela says that Sergeant Redfern waved— waved—from inside the pump house; this same pump house that had a wall between the pump house and the hide-site; that blocked the view of people in the pump house of the hide-site.

None of them remember a consistent timeline. They're all sticking to different versions, different parts, of Staff Sergeant Hensley's original cover story for this murder. And we know that murder happened on 11 May 2007.

And let's talk about security. These soldiers, they're snipers; they think they're cool. They have one guy on security that morning, early that morning; they had one guy on security and four asleep. Suddenly a man walks in, unmolested, into their hide-site and they say, "Oh, God, we've got to have 100 percent security."

Well, no, because Sergeant Hand is still on that berm asleep. So what do you have? You have Sergeant Vela and Staff Sergeant Hensley in the hide-site, if you're going to believe this story; Sergeant Hand asleep on the berm; Sergeant Redfern and the accused completely out of sight with no connection, no communication, out in this pump house. Is that adequate security? Is that what would have been done had this gone on in that hide-site? That does not make sense. Especially when you remember the testimony of Specialist Myrom: they're all out, they're all exposed, they're all out there in that hide-site when he arrives with his group to start conducting SSE. they're just out there. They go on and on and on about how this is a dangerous area and yet they are all exposed out there with this body there; they're all exposed. It does not make sense.

Defense also talked about sniper tactics. It doesn't matter. It doesn't matter. When you have a target 100 meters from you, you don't have to be a sniper to take that target out. You don't have to use sniper tactics. You don't have to use sniper tactics to murder someone from 100 meters. You don't have to use sniper tactics—you don't have to be a sniper to plant wire on remains. And you certainly don't have to be a sniper to shoot someone in the head with a 9mm from a few inches—to conduct a close kill, much less put an AK-47 on the body.

And let's talk about that AK-47. You will read in Specialist Sandoval's statement that the night before, he hears a conversation in the presence of Staff Sergeant Hensley, Sergeant Hand, Sergeant Vela, and Sergeant Redfern; somebody says, "Who's got the AK-47?" And you also heard evidence that they don't normally take AK-47s or wire out on missions; they don't. Why would they have that AK-47?

What you need to focus on is what was in the accused's mind on 27 April 2007 when he shot—when he murdered that man. All he saw was a man cutting grass. Read his statement. He did not see a hostile act, he did not see a hostile intent; all this individual was doing was squatting in a field cutting grass. And he plants wire on the remains.

On 11 May 2007, what's important is where Sandoval was, which will tell you what he was doing. At the end of the day, the government is confident that you will find the accused guilty of all offenses charged.

FIFTEEN - THE VERDICT

"There are several matters which you should consider in determining an appropriate sentence. You should bear in mind that our society recognizes five principal reasons for the sentence of those who violate the law. They are rehabilitation of the wrongdoer, punishment of the wrongdoer, protection of society from the wrongdoer, preservation of good order and discipline in the military, and deterrence of the wrongdoer and those who know of his crime and his sentence from committing the same or similar offenses. The weight to be given any or all of these reasons, along with all other sentencing matters in this case, rests solely within your discretion."

~ **Sentencing Instruction 2-5-21,**
Department of the Army Pamphlet 27-9

Sandoval was facing two counts of murder, one premeditated and one unpremeditated. The first charge sheet stated:

Charge I: Violation of the UCMJ, Article 118... The Specification: *In that Specialist Jorge G. Sandoval, Jr., did, at or near Abu Shemsi, Iraq, on or about 27 April, 2007, murder an Iraqi national by means of shooting him with a rifle.*

Charge II: Violation of the UCMJ, Article 134...The Specification: *In that Specialist Jorge G. Sandoval, Jr., did, at or near Jurf as Sakhr, Iraq, on or about 11 May, 2007, wrongfully place command wire with the remains of Genei Nesir Khudair Al-Janabi, which conduct was to the prejudice of good order and discipline in the armed forces or of a nature to bring discredit upon the armed forces.*

On the charge of murder related to 27 April, the charge sheet did not state whether or not Sandoval was charged with premeditated murder, so the fallback was unpremeditated murder, or simply murder.

The second charge sheet stated as follows:

Additional Charge I: Violation of the UCMJ, Article 118...The Specification: *In that Specialist Jorge G. Sandoval, Jr., U.S. Army, did, at or near Jurf as Sakhr, Iraq, on or about 11 May 2007, with premeditation, murder Genei Nesir Khudair Al-Janabi by means of shooting him with a 9mm pistol.*

Additional Charge II: Violation of the UCMJ, Article 92...

Specification 1:

In that Specialist Jorge G. Sandoval, Jr., U.S. Army, who knew of his duties, at or near Jurf as Sakhr, Iraq, on or about 11 May 2007, was derelict in the performance of his duties in that he failed to ensure the humane treatment of a detainee, as it was his duty to do.

Specification 2: *In that Specialist Jorge G. Sandoval, Jr., U.S. Army, who knew of his duties, at or near Jurf as Sakhr, Iraq, and at or near Forward Operating Base Iskandariyah, Iraq, from between on or about 11 May 2007 and on or about 27 June 2007, was derelict in the performance of those duties in that he willfully failed to report the murder of a detainee, as it was his duty to do.*

Additional Charge III: Violation of the UCMJ, Article 134...Specification:

In that Jorge G. Sandoval, Jr., U.S. Army, did, at or near Jurf as Sakhr, Iraq, on or about 11 May 2007, wrongfully place an AK-47 rifle with the remains of Genei Nesir Khudair Al-Janabi, which conduct was to the prejudice of the good order and discipline in the armed forces or of a nature to bring discredit upon the armed forces.

For the 27 April 2007 murder charge, the maximum punishment Sandoval was facing was zero to life without eligibility for parole.

For the 11 May 2007 premeditated murder charge, Sandoval was facing a mandatory minimum of imprisonment for life without eligibility for parole. Given that the Charge Sheet for the 11 May charge was premeditated murder, death was a possible sentence. However, the prosecutors would have had to have given notice to the defense that they were seeking death and they did not do so. Thus, the maximum punishment Sandoval was facing was life without the eligibility for parole.

For the charges of murder and premeditated murder on both Charge Sheets combined, Sandoval was facing:

- reduction in rank to E-1 (the lowest rank)
- total forfeiture of all pay and allowances
- a dishonorable discharge from the Army, and
- life in prison without the eligibility for parole

Generally speaking, for the non-murder charges, Sandoval was facing the following:

For the two dereliction of duty charges, Article 92, UCMJ:

- reduction to the grade of Private E-1
- forfeiture of all pay and allowances
- confinement for six months for each charge, (thus one year total for the combined charges)
- and a bad conduct discharge from the Army.

For the command wire, Article 134 UCMJ, he was facing:

- reduction to the grade of Private E-1

- forfeiture of all pay and allowances
- confinement for five years, and
- a dishonorable discharge from the Army

For the AK-47, Article 134 UCMJ:

- reduction to the grade of Private E-1
- forfeiture of all pay and allowances
- confinement for five years, and
- a dishonorable discharge from the Army

On 28 September 2007 after three days of trial, a military panel found Sandoval guilty of one specification of a general Article 134 offense of wrongfully placing command wire on the body of an unknown deceased on 27 April 2007. For the one charge he was ultimately convicted of, Sandoval faced:

- reduction to the grade of Private E-1
- forfeiture of all pay and allowances
- confinement for five years
- and a dishonorable discharge from the Army

This was a disputed point given some vagueness about the wording of the charge; however, the judge ultimately instructed the jury that the above was the maximum punishment that Sandoval was facing after he was found guilty.

At trial, Sandoval had faced five actual charges, with one of them having two separate specifications.[42] The panel found Sandoval not guilty of four of the five charges he faced at trial, as follows:

---

42   Under the UCMJ a charge can have more than one specification. For example, Sandoval was charged with two specifications of a charge of dereliction of duty in violation of Article 92 of the UCMJ. It is essentially charging him with two separate dereliction of duty allegations, but instead of saying two charges, it is referred to simply as the charge of dereliction of duty with two specifications. If convicted of both specifications the potential punishments would be double.

- murdering an unknown deceased on 27 April 2007;

- murdering, with premeditation, an unknown deceased on 11 May 2007;

- dereliction of duty by failing to ensure the humane treatment of a detainee on 11 May 2007;

- and wrongfully placing an AK-47 on an unknown deceased on 11 May 2007.

The Additional Charge II, Specification 2, alleging that Sandoval was derelict in his duties for not reporting the murder of the detainee on 11 May 2007 was dismissed by the military judge at the request of the defense. It was unconstitutional to charge Sandoval with murder and then also charge him with not reporting the murder to the authorities. Hence, it was a violation of Sandoval's Fifth Amendment right against self-incrimination and his right to remain silent when being questioned about a potential crime.

Before the military panel sentenced Sandoval, I wanted to give them a look at him as a person. So, we took his unsworn statement in front of the panel, the purpose of which was to personalize the defendant. As Sandoval had not testified at trial, this was the first time the panel had a chance to hear him speak. I wanted them to hear him say in his own words that he was sorry for his actions and to have the opportunity to tell the panel some things about his life.

As the statement was unsworn, the prosecutors could not cross-examine him about the statement. He simply got to talk.

Captain Claudio took his statement, as follows:

(Q: DEFENSE COUNSEL, ADC)

(A: SPC SANDOVAL)

Q: Specialist Sandoval, how long have you been in the

Army?

A: Sir, I've been in the Army a little over three years. About three years and two months now, sir.

Q: And you went into the Army through the MEPS station in Fort Sam Houston?

A: Yes, I did, sir. Back in 2004, sir.

Q: And is that your hometown?

A: Yes, it is, sir.

Q: And where are you from?

A: Laredo, Texas, sir.

Q: And have you lived there your whole life?

A: Yes, I have, sir. Up until I joined the Army, sir.

Q: How old are you now?

A: I'm 22-years old, sir.

Q: Did you like growing up in Laredo, Texas?

A: Yes—yes, I did, sir. Rather interesting growing up along the border to Mexico.

Q: Go ahead.

A: I had family in Mexico and we drove over and saw them.

Q: And did you have a normal childhood?

A: Yes, sir, for the most part. A little fight here and there with the sister, but you know, sibling rivalry. A regular childhood, sir.

Q: How many sisters do you have?

A: Two, sir.

Q: Closer to either one of them?

A: Yes, the oldest, sir, my sister, Norma.

Q: And Norma tried to come over here for your court-martial?

A: Yes, she did, sir. She attempted twice, sir.

Q: Were there some issues over at the Kuwaiti airport?

A: Yes, some issues with her documentation, sir. She has a Mexican passport, sir. I can't really—I don't know what the issue was, sir.

Q: But it would be fair to say they wouldn't let her in?

A: They—yes, sir, they wouldn't let her in.

Q: During the time that you were growing up, did you ever play any sports or anything like that?

A: Yes, sir. When I was twelve or thirteen years old, I played basketball at a local church. I had a lot of fun.

Q: During the time you were actually in high school, you did JROTC?

A: Yes, I did, sir, four years.

Q: How did you like that?

A: It was awesome. I loved it.

Q: What types of things did you do?

A: Well, upon arriving on my freshman year, I was fourteen, we were issued a uniform. The uniform I'm not wearing today, sir, Class A's. We had inspections on every Friday. I was part of numerous skills teams, my favorite being the Army drill team. It was kind of like the Old Guard. We went to compete all over Texas, sir.

Q: Did you ever get any awards or anything like that?

A: Yes, sir. Challenge coins and numerous ribbons.

Q: Did that affect your desire to come into the Army?

A: Yes, sir.

Q: Why did you join?

A: I joined—it was just one thing I always wanted to do, sir. Something that I felt that I needed to do, sir. This country has been very good to my family, sir, and [the accused's voice began breaking up and he began to tear up].

ADC: Take your time.

A: [The accused's voice was broken and he became tearful.] Just growing up, sir—I mean, my mother, she emigrated from Mexico—I mean, this country's just been very good to us, sir. I just felt like I had to do something, sir.

ADC: Take your time.

[Long pause while the accused regained control of his emotions.]

ADC: Ready to continue?

Q: Yes, sir.

A: Where did you go to Basic?

Q: I went to Basic at Fort Benning, Georgia, sir.

A: How did you like that?

A: Very interesting, sir. I'd never seen so many hills, sir. Coming from Texas—South Texas is a very flat part of the state of Texas, sir. I'd just never seen so many hills, sir. I'd never walked as much, and overall it was just a very great experience for me and that's where I became a soldier, sir. That's where I was taught to take care of the man next to me, sir.

Q: What types of things did you learn in Infantry Basic?

A: Everything from taking care of your equipment, sir, maintaining your weapon system, firing different weapon systems, sir. Squad movements, road marches, medical aid, sir.

Q: Now did you do AIT[43] there as well?

A: Yes, I did, sir. Basic and infantry. It's just a combination of them both—integrated.

Q: And eventually you went to Airborne School?

A: Yes, I did, sir.

Q: How did that happen?

A: About six weeks into being at basic training, sir, our drill sergeants came up to our platoon and they asked if anyone wanted to volunteer for Airborne School or Ranger School. I had a friend—I had a couple of friends that were paratroopers before. When they graduated, sir, they just told me that it was the most awesome thing they had ever done, sir. So, based on my performance and my physical condition, sir, I was allowed to receive a contract for Airborne School, sir.

Q: And how did you like jumping?

A: It's the best thing I've ever done, sir. I love it. The second time I was on an airplane, I was jumping out of it, sir. I had never been on an airplane before, except for the fact when I flew to Georgia. But that—the second time I was on an airplane, I was jumping out of it, sir, and it was one of the most awesome experiences I've—I had never dreamed of doing anything like that, sir. I didn't know I could do something like that, sir.

Q: How many times have you gone on jumps?

A: About eighteen jumps, sir. From the time I trained at Fort Benning and the time I've jumped in Alaska, sir.

Q: And is that where your unit is currently stationed,

---

43   AIT, or Advanced Individual Training, is the school where a soldier goes to learn their specific follow-on training related to their individual job after basic training. In the case of Sandoval and members of his unit, this was training for being an infantryman and took place at Fort Benning, Georgia.

in Alaska?

A: Yes, sir. We're out of Fort Richardson, sir.

Q: How did you get to Fort Richardson? Was there something that they decided that you were going to be stationed there? Was there only a certain amount of airborne units?

A: Well, during basic training, I was what was called uncommitted, sir. And upon receiving our contracts, me and a couple of friends just looked on a roster and it said Alaska and airborne. We all being from southern states, we just got nervous, we didn't know what to expect, sir. It was Alaska, sir.

Q: And how do you like Alaska?

A: I love it, sir. I'd never seen snow before in my life, sir. It's just—it's beautiful, sir. One of the most beautiful places I've ever seen, sir.

Q: And how do you like being an infantryman in Alaska?

A: I love it, sir. The training is much more challenging and demanding. Walking through the snow isn't just like walking on the street, sir. It puts you to the test a lot, sir. It's just an awesome experience to be able to do those things, sir.

Q: And how do you like being in the 1st of the 501st?

A: I love it, sir. Some of the best people that I know, I met in the 501st, sir. I know I'll never forget them, sir.

Q: When did you finally come here to Iraq?

A: That was in October of '06, sir.

Q: And do you remember when you actually got notification that you were coming?

A: I believe in August, sir, of '06.

Q: How did your family feel?

A: They were afraid, sir. I can't blame them. It's a war, sir.

Q: And what type of missions have you gone on, other than the ones obviously that you've heard about over the course of the trial? Could you just describe a little bit of them so that the members can hear about them?

A: All kinds of reconnaissance missions, sir. Observation, intelligence gathering, sir—long periods of time in areas where—like hot spots, sir—areas where there was intel that there were bad people doing bad things, sir.

Q: Now you have a Combat Infantry Badge?

A: Yes, I do, sir.

Q: How did you initially get that badge?

A: Me and a couple of members from my platoon were on a recon mission, sir. Upon EXFIL⁴⁴ we decided to go check an area. I believe our Platoon Leader had seen something over by the bongos, sir. So, we decided to go check it out, sir, and it was in the morning—I believe it was the 21ˢᵗ of February, sir. Upon reaching the area, we discovered that there was nothing there, sir, so we started to head back to our vehicles, sir. We stopped to take a quick couple of pictures of this—of this bridge that was supposedly going to be destroyed by the ODA (ordinance or explosive) teams on a follow up. So we're taking pictures and gathering intelligence on this bridge—this bridge was mostly used for—intel suggested that this bridge was used for trafficking of weapons and munitions, sir. Upon completion of taking

---

44   *Extraction, EXFIL, or exfiltration is the process of removing personnel when it is considered imperative that they be immediately relocated from a hostile environment and taken to a secure area.

photos of this bridge, we were walking back to our vehicles and we received—we received fire—sniper fire, sir. I had tripped, sir. The ground broke in front of me, sir. And as I looked up, I saw everyone behind the trucks already trying for cover and a round went over my head, sir, and hit in pretty close proximity, sir.

Q: The last couple of days, you've obviously been being court-martialed here on charges of murder. Before that happened, was your family aware of the situation?

A: Yes, sir.

Q: And did you ever talk to them about this?

A: Yes, I did, sir.

[The accused's voice began to break up again and he became tearful again.]

Q: And how do they feel about what's happened to you?

A: They all supported me, sir. They all said don't give up and they never lost faith, sir.

Q: When was the last time you talked to your mother?

A: I can't remember, sir.

Q: And why is that?

A: I've been in confinement for about ninety-five days now, sir. Well, my mother does not—she doesn't speak English, sir. So—they won't let us—over at the confinement facility, they won't let us talk in any other language other than English there, sir. So I haven't been able to speak to her, sir.

Q: Have you talked to your sisters—obviously, your sister was going to come here and your father wrote?

A: Yes, sir.

Q: Has there been any media coverage in your

hometown regarding this?

A: Yes, sir.

Q: And some of this media coverage has obviously painted you as a murderer?

A: Yes, sir.

[The accused's voice continued to be broken and he remained tearful.]

A: I was told it was all over the papers, sir. I personally didn't see any of it, sir. I was in confinement during all of this.

Q: And does your family have reporters come to their house and ask them questions?

A: Yes, sir. My sister warned me that my family was being called on a daily basis, sir, harassing them. Basically, they would call them nonstop, sir. That kind of thing, sir.

Q: Specialist Sandoval, do you want to stay in the Army?

A: Yes, I do, sir.

Q: Why do you want to stay in the Army?

A: It's the one thing that I strived to do, sir. It's the "thing" that I wanted to do, sir. I don't want to even think of it being taken away, sir.

Q: One of the panel's options is to discharge you; it's what we just talked about it. Is there any reason that you can give them to keep you in? Is there anything else that you have to say?

A: Yes, sir. I would ask that I be allowed to stay in the military, sir—in the Army, sir. It's what I've wanted to do my entire life, sir. I just—I really don't see myself doing anything else, sir. I don't—I just don't see myself—the Army is my life, sir.

Q: You've been found guilty of placing command wire by the panel here today—excuse me, yesterday. Do you take responsibility for those actions?

A: Yes, I do, sir. I take full responsibility for my actions. I'm a man, sir. First and foremost, I would like to apologize for the mistake—for the mistakes that I've made, for the errors in judgment that I made [the accused's voice began to crack again and his eyes became tearful] that I made. Just the anguish that I've caused to a lot of people and I'm pretty sure that you, Mr. President, and the panel would have had better things to do today. I just—everyone that's here, I would just like to apologize to everyone.

Q: What about your chain of command?

A: Especially my chain of command. I feel like I let them down, sir. I don't know what else—I just want to be allowed the chance to prove myself and that I can be—that I can be a better person, sir, a better soldier, sir.

ADC:Thank you very much, Specialist Sandoval, you can be seated now.

[The accused resumed his seat at the defense table.]

SIXTEEN - SENTENCING

Zeus gave Pandora a box and told her that under no circumstances to open the box. However, owing to her insatiable curiosity, Pandora cracked the lid. Out of the box flew every trouble known to humanity—strife, sickness, toil and ills all escaped to afflict forevermore. Pandora managed to trap one last spirit in the box as she shut the lid. What remained was hope.

*~ **Hesiod, Greek Mythology***

The military judge dismissed the panel and a closed hearing between the judge and all counsel was held. The Judge talked to us about the sentencing guideline instructions he intended to give the panel. Then the judge reopened the hearing, re-seated the panel, and allowed Sandoval to continue his unsworn statement by reading a letter from his mother, written in Spanish.

During the reading of the letter, Sandoval alternated between reading in Spanish and in English as there were no Spanish language court interpreters present at the trial. By having Sandoval read the letter in both Spanish and English, it highlighted that his mother was a Mexican citizen and that he had decided to enlist and serve and defend the new country of citizenship of his family.

As he read this letter from his mother, Sandoval's voice broke.

To whom it may concern, I am Elisa Sandoval, mother of my son, Jorge Sandoval, Jr. Jorge has and has always been a good person. We never had any problems with him. He would always—he had always behaved himself well. He is a very good son. He always participated in the activities at school. My son is innocent. Elisa Sandoval, mother of Jorge Sandoval, Jr.

The words from the letter were simple and powerful as it was a mother's plea for mercy for her son that she wrote before the conviction. Hearing his mother's words from a proud combat tested soldier's mouth was awe-inspiring. Once Sandoval read the letter, with tears beginning to swell in the back of Sandoval's eyes, as well as mine and Captain Claudio's, we rested our case.

We were also permitted to present to the jury a "Good Soldier Book," which was comprised of pictures, certificates, and letters written on Sandoval's behalf from his friends and family back home in Texas with the hopes of further personalizing him to the jury. Obviously, because the trial was held in Iraq, Sandoval's friends and family were unable to attend in person.

The purpose of the letters was to show the jury that Sandoval was a good soldier, a good person, and a productive member of society. We also knew that providing letters of support could impact a juror by causing them to reflect upon the impact that any sentence might have on others—not just on Sandoval. A Good Soldier Book was extremely important as you never know how you are going to impact a juror and one letter, or one sentence in a letter, may strike a chord with a juror as the reason to be lenient.

We were asking for leniency and mercy. The panel had just denied the prosecutors their convictions for murder and there was always the possibility that as a conciliatory gesture to the prosecutors, the panel could impose a harsh sentence on Sandoval for what would typically be a very minor conviction.

The Good Soldier Book contained the following letters, some of which have been edited slightly for the sake of brevity or clarity.

SERGEANT MAJOR VEHON LOCKLEAR, JR., U.S. ARMY, RETIRED, SENIOR ARMY INSTRUCTOR, JROTC, MARTIN HIGH SCHOOL,

I have had the distinct pleasure and honor to be acquainted with Jorge Sandoval since 2000. Jorge joined the JROTC program...during his first year in high school and remained there for four years. I remember when he arrived, his eagerness and great interest in the program was just amazing...

Jorge always wore the uniform with so much pride and admiration for the JROTC and the U.S. Army. His uniform was always cleaned and neatly pressed and starched for all inspections and competitions. He looked like a seasoned soldier even before joining the Army...

This man displayed unlimited leadership potential and was a great role model for the other cadets to emulate...

It is with great sadness that I have to write this letter of moral character for Jorge Sandoval under these circumstances. It is also a great pleasure for me to write this letter and to share his many great accomplishments in the JROTC program with you and his chain of command. He is a young man of great character and many honorable qualities as a soldier and a human being...We are here to support him 100 percent of the way."

◆ ◆ ◆

CESAR D. SAAVEDRA

I am one of Jorge G. Sandoval's closest friends. I have known Jorge for almost thirteen years now. He was my best friend during our childhood and I am grateful to have met him. As you all should know by now, we grew up in the poor side of town which many call "the ghetto." In many places like that, there are bad things people can get into if they're not mentally strong. I can say I was one of the weak ones. I was hanging out with the wrong crowds and doing things I shouldn't be doing at that age. I can still remember Jorge telling me over and over to stay out of trouble, stop hanging with the bad crowds, and telling me that wasn't a life for me.

Now that I look back, it is kind of ironic because I am nearly two years older than him. Ever since I've known him, I have considered him to be my younger brother. Jorge has always been a very mature person. A few years after I met Jorge, I took his advice to stop doing things I shouldn't be doing.

I can still remember how after school we hung out at his house to play video games and play with his toy soldiers. As long as I can remember, Jorge's dream was to be in the United States Army. He used to talk to my father about it because he served proudly in the United States Army.

Jorge's father would take us to his godfather's ranch. Jorge would always ask his father to buy him a lot of Army stuff; he had all kinds of things. We would go out to the woods to play Army with our paint guns. My family could never provide me with things like that but Jorge would always give me things so I could have my own. Jorge was the kind of person that liked to go out and spend money with me, knowing I never had any. He's the kind of person that if he has one dollar in his pocket and someone else needs it, he'll gladly give that dollar without thinking twice about it.

So in high school, I joined the football team and Jorge of course joined the JROTC… I used to go to his house after school and see him practicing his moves with the rifle for the color guard team. He was the best at it. After high school, Jorge enlisted in the United States Army and I can say I was very proud of my little brother. I have always respected and loved Jorge for the person he is. He always sets goals in life and accomplishes them. He makes you think about what a person can do with his life.

After he was shipped to Alaska, I started to make my own goals in life, and now I own a small business and have my own family. I can proudly say Jorge is responsible for my life change. I've always introduced Jorge as the person who saved my life. I can say he saved my life because many of the people I grew up with are either in jail or deceased...

So, this is the main reason I am having a difficult time believing Jorge is a life-taking person—because he saved my life so many times...

◆ ◆ ◆

ASHLEY GARCIA

My name is Ashley Garcia. My fiancé, Cesar, is Jorge's best friend. Jorge is going to be the best man in our wedding, and for my fiancé there has been no other choice. I have been with my fiancé for eight years, so I have known Jorge for eight years. Thinking back on the day I met Jorge, I can remember my fiancé being excited for us to meet. He was introduced to me as the person who saved my fiancé's life on more than one occasion.

You see, Jorge was a person who tried to stay out of trouble even though the neighborhood they grew up in was full of people and things that put them right in the middle of it. My fiancé could possibly not be with me right now. Jorge gave us the opportunity to meet and have a beautiful life and son together.

I have known Jorge to be a great person and a big part of our lives; he is a part of our family. I have always seen Jorge just as he is—a person who is outgoing, funny, caring, and most of all responsible. Jorge to me is such a strong person.

Since I can remember, Jorge had always wanted to serve in the Army. It was his dream, and I have always admired him so much for doing what he needed to do to make that dream come true. Something not a lot of people do. Actually, we always told him not to go, but be always said, "No, it's what I want." It was the only thing I think he was sure of.

I got to see him while in school. I can remember seeing him in the parade in his school's ROTC, following orders and marching down the street. When he graduated I was there, happy to share that moment with him, knowing that he was that much closer to his dream and being sad to know that soon he would go...

I can remember him being so excited the day he was to leave and from that moment on, we have been counting the days left until he comes home for good. We have worked our wedding around to be able to have Jorge there. Without a doubt, you could say that he is one of the reasons we have waited. We wanted to be sure that he could be there because, as I said, if it were not for him, there may not have been a wedding. So, of course, there would not be one without him.

Jorge to me is a giving person not a taking one. He gives without thinking of what he gets in return. And for me, Jorge has given me the greatest gift of all, a friend and a family.

◆ ◆ ◆

RAMON R. ELIZONDO

I have known Jorge Sandoval Jr. in a variety of capacities since birth. He has been my son's friend for the past several years. In addition, he is my longtime friend Jorge Sandoval Sr.'s son.

When I heard of Jr.'s dilemma on the news, I was shocked. Mainly because Jr. has always been a good kid and could not be capable of doing what he is being accused of. Jr. excelled in high school and was a member of the Army ROTC for four years. Upon graduating, he chose to serve his country and join the United States Army. He chose to do something that many men do not have the guts to do.

In summary, I highly recommend that Jr. is treated fairly and given every chance possible to defend himself.

♦ ♦ ♦

CARLOS AND ROGELIO GARAY

We are both Vietnam veterans and have known Jorge Sandoval, Jr. since he was a child. He and his family used to live in the same neighborhood where we lived. We were able to watch him grow up and turn into a fine young man, and always knew that he performed well in school. We often encouraged him to join the military after graduating from high school. It was an honor when we were informed that he had enlisted and was part of the Airborne Division serving in Iraq.

We strongly feel that Jorge Sandoval, Jr., is a young man of good character who is innocent of the crime he has been accused of.

♦ ♦ ♦

ROGELIO BETANCOURT

I'm writing this letter in reference to Jorge Sandoval, a very good friend of mine that I've known for nine years, since he was a freshman at Martin High School in Laredo, Texas. I met him when I joined the ROTC program. In all the years that I have known him, he has never gotten into any trouble with the law.

While in high school, he was very involved in ROTC, constantly participating in the various teams the program had. He was a member of the Armed Drill Team, the Physical Fitness Team, the Rifle Team, and the Color Guard, constantly in practice after school. He took a lot of pride in his uniform appearance, always trying to outdo himself and others in numerous things. Out of school, he was always trying to be physically fit to be ready for when he would join the Army.

With his friends, he was always giving us advice and very optimistic; with his family, he was very fond of his mother and his two sisters Norma and Sandra, including their kids, and was very close and loving to his father.

Jorge Sandoval has always been eager to serve his country with pride and honor. He's always wanted to be a war hero and to lead men with desires as big as his to defend the constitution of the United States of America…

In all, I know this man's exemplary behavior should be followed by a lot of the citizens in this country.

◆ ◆ ◆

CARMEN CONTRERAS, SUPERVISOR, TEXAS HEALTH & HUMAN SERVICES COMMISSION

"I am preparing this letter with my most sincere wish that it will help Jorge. I have known Jorge Sandoval, Jr., for many years, since he was a young boy attending elementary school. He has, since then, always had a good attitude toward life, happy, having fun in simple ways. He was always a good young boy and now a good and responsible young adult. He is kind of quiet but at the same time, he communicates well enough…

He is very respectful and always saying hello with a big smile. I know him as being fair with everybody and treating everybody with respect, never trying to do any harm to anybody.

He loves to listen to music, as well as watch a good

movie and as I previously mentioned, he enjoys the simple pleasures in life. During his school years, he was part of the famous and proud All City Choir. His collection of music CDs is vast, from Mexican music, romantic music, as well as country music. Somebody like Jorge enjoying the simple pleasure of listening to music is incapable of any wrongdoing.

When I first met Jorge, he was a young boy and at such a young age he demonstrated being a responsible U.S. citizen. His father would every other week take him to an Army/Navy store and he would always find some little gadget to buy—a handkerchief, a cap, a set of inexpensive binoculars—always displaying his ambition of joining the Army and serving his country.

Let me assure you that I believe Jorge could not possibly do any of the things that are mentioned in the media. I have talked to Jorge and he has assured me he did no wrongdoing. I have known him for a long time. I know he is being truthful.

I hope that this letter serves its purpose, which is that people know him better, that they will be able to see that Jorge is a good young man, who deserves all of the good things in life. Thanking you in advance for taking time to read this letter.

◆ ◆ ◆

KARLA ALEJANDRA VASQUEZ

I'm the niece of Jorge Sandoval. My uncle is a really nice person. He has always been there for me and everything I've needed. He has helped me and taught me many things. I also learned to have courage and help other people from him because he was doing that in Iraq!

He is also a fun person to be with. He was in ROTC at the school which I attend now. He was taught to do things the right way and never do wrong. Every time I and my brother are with him, he teaches us new things about life, and to never do bad things! I think what they're doing to him is wrong. I know it's my word against the people who think he did wrong. But, I know that my uncle wouldn't do anything wrong and I swear witness to that fact. My parents weren't the only ones who taught me how to do right from wrong or show my manners.

I'm proud of my uncle for what he has done. He has showed strength, courage, but mainly endurance. This is why I say I'm proud of my uncle very much!

◆ ◆ ◆

JORGE G. SANDOVAL, SR.

What can a father say about his son? I can say and swear on my mother's grave that Jorge has never given me any problems as a child and now as an adult he is well mannered and well behaved. He is a loving son, a loving brother, a good friend, and a caring uncle. You can ask anybody on my block who knows Jorge and they will tell you the same. I am proud to call him son!

As a child, he would play with his toy soldiers and would dream of becoming a good soldier for the United States Army. I am talking about a young man that decided to leave all his loved ones behind to serve his country and serve it well. Now all his hopes and dreams are coming down on him.

SEVENTEEN · CLEMENCY

"The accused may submit to the convening authority any matters that may reasonably tend to affect the convening authority's decision whether to disapprove any findings of guilty or to approve the sentence."

**~ Rule for Courts-Martial 1105,
Uniform Code of Military Justice**

Sandoval's character, combined with all of the testimony we had presented, let the truth shine out. On 29 September 2007, Sandoval was sentenced to be reduced to private (E-2), to be confined for 150 days and to forfeit all pay and allowances during his confinement. While the formal sentence had been announced, there will still a number of legal issues to be addressed by the military judge.

With regard to sentencing credit and the Article 13 pretrial punishment issue, the military judge ruled as follows:

I conclude that prohibiting the wearing of rank on the ACU's was not done with a punitive intent or purpose; however, I find that, under the circumstances, this condition is more rigorous than required to run the facility. Good order and discipline are required to run a confinement facility safely and effectively. The interaction between cadre and inmates, and the interaction among inmates, are all part of that. Inmates have to follow the orders of cadre, regardless of rank. This is true regardless of whether the inmates wear their rank. Taking their rank off of the uniform does not change their rank.

A facility can issue an order that inmates cannot give orders to other inmates, or exercise any authority over other inmates. In some facilities, it may assist in good order if the inmates did not wear their rank so that there is less tension between inmates. That could reasonably serve a valid non-punitive purpose.

However, in this case, it appears that all of the inmates know everyone's rank, regardless of whether they wear it. That is evident from the testimony of Specialist Sandoval. I already stated that there may be a valid non-punitive purpose, but I must weigh that against how rigorous the condition is.

In this case, in the circumstances at this confinement facility, it is more rigorous because the inmates wear ACU's and not a uniform that would not require rank.

It is a fact in the Army, that for ACU's, no rank is equal to the rank of E-1. Therefore, the inmates must wear the uniform of an E-1 while in pretrial confinement. The United States Court of Appeals for the Armed Forces has stated, "reduction in rank is a well-established punishment, which unlawfully imposed warrants sentence relief."

Also, I note that I was open to the argument that ACU's are required rather than jumpsuits or some other uniform because of the deployed nature of this particular confinement facility. But no evidence was presented on that. I even asked Lieutenant Commander Zinc if that was the reason and he said that it was not.

In summary, forcing pretrial inmates to wear the uniform of an E-1 was more rigorous than required to operate the confinement facility. That condition of pretrial confinement violated Article 13. The work details did not violate Article 13.

Thus, the military judge ordered that Sandoval be credited with ninety-six days of pretrial confinement credit [28 June 2007 to 29 September 2007] and ten days of Article 13 credit for being illegally punished while in pretrial confinement.

♦ ♦ ♦

When a general court-martial is concluded, the entire recording is transcribed and the transcript and exhibits are compiled into a Record of Trial. That record is served on the accused and his defense counsel, and they are then able to submit "clemency matters" to the General who convened the court for consideration.

The submission can contain "any matters that reasonably tend to affect the convening authority's decision whether to disapprove any findings of guilty or to approve the sentence… submissions may include allegations of errors affecting the legality of the findings or sentence; portions or summaries of the record and copies of documentary evidence offered or introduced at trial; matters in mitigation which were not available for consideration at the court-martial; and clemency recommendations by any member, the military judge, or any other person…"

The clemency process is in the UCMJ as a "check and balance" on the court-martial proceedings. This is an opportunity for the General Officer who convened the court and moved forward with the charges to evaluate the result and theoretically fix any errors or injustices in the proceedings or result. In practice, most General Officers simply affirm any convictions and sentences, and I truly doubt that they read the majority of clemency submissions. However, in certain cases they will provide some clemency relief from the conviction or sentence. As such, a defense attorney should never disregard the clemency process and should attempt with a full effort to somehow trigger something within the commander's mindset to get relief.

A few months after the trial, I received in the mail eight large, bound stacks of paper that were the Record of Trial. I prepared a thirteen-page clemency submission and asked MG Lynch to "disapprove the Court's finding of guilty, disapprove all punishments, and restore SPC Sandoval to the position he was in prior to referral of charges in this case."

I outlined some errors in the advice that the General was given by his legal advisor, the Staff Judge Advocate. I argued that "the order given by Captain Matthew Didier on 27 April 2007 to his snipers to engage insurgents who were fleeing in the snipers' direction was a lawful order and the military judge improperly instructed that the order was unlawful." I outlined the events leading up to the order and that Didier had relayed the order to Hensley who relayed it to Sandoval. I outlined that during the trial, the military judge determined, as a matter of law, that the order given by Didier was unlawful and instructed the panel as such. This was an incorrect determination as the order complied with the Rules of Engagement (ROE) for that unit and that mission.

I stated as follows:

All witnesses who testified at the trial about what ROE was in effect and what it was testified that it came from CPT Didier's mouth and his determinations. It was not an ROE that came from higher or was set by some senior command. CPT Didier testified that his order to shoot was in compliance with the ROE as he knew it and as he set. He authorized the killing of an insurgent and that order was in compliance with the ROE.

The fact that the deceased was an enemy insurgent was seemingly un-contradicted by the prosecution during the trial as they stipulated to testimony that an Iraqi Intelligence Officer examined the body of the deceased on 27 April 2007 and identified him as being an insurgent who had attacked U.S. and Iraqi forces earlier that morning. As such, the order by CPT Didier to kill an insurgent who had attacked U.S. and Iraqi forces was a lawful order and the military judge improperly instructed the panel that it was an unlawful order.

CPT Didier testified about the ROE as follows:

Q: Defense Counsel: And you're talking about the

ROE, in addition to the brief from Major DiMigleo [the unit's JAG attorney] before you went—before you deployed, you also received an additional briefing on the ROE in the form of OPDs, correct?

A: Yes.

Q: And in those OPDs, scenarios were talked about, correct?

A: Yes.

And it was within the ROEs that you understood and the ROEs that were briefed to Specialist Sandoval that if somebody attacked and then fled and dropped their weapon, that they were still a legitimate target up to the point that they had not surrendered or were injured, correct?

A: Yes.

Q: And that was based on those OPDs and that was communicated to Specialist Sandoval, correct?

A: Yes.

[We'll return now to my clemency letter.]

What ROE was the military judge referring to? We'll assume the military judge was relying on the general study and classes on ROE only generally taught by Army judge advocates. However, this generalized textbook version of the ROE was not admitted into evidence in this case and was not the ROE that was controlling on 27 April 2007. Thus, the military judge's reliance on an ROE that was not in evidence and was not controlling was improper. However, although it is unclear whether the record supports this assumption, even if the military judge was relying on the ROE set by CPT Didier and even if he made the determination that CPT Didier's order to shoot based on his own ROE was unlawful, this determination is still flawed as his rationale does not follow the presumption in the law that all orders are lawful. [Reference to ROT, Page 366.] Thus, the starting point in the legal analysis should have been the presumption that the order was lawful. The military judge clearly did not follow this presumption.

Though SPC Sandoval was not convicted of murder when he shot and killed the mortar team member by following that order, the order to shoot thereby labeling the mortar team member and deceased as hostile was directly related to SPC Sandoval's later action of placing command wire on the body of the insurgent—the unknown deceased. SPC Sandoval thought everything was lawful that day. SPC Sandoval thought the order to kill the mortar team member was lawful. In fact, it was lawful.

By improperly stating the law in the findings instructions given to the panel, the Military Judge shifted the burden from the government to the defense to show the reasonableness of SPC Sandoval's actions. Additionally, this incorrect instruction tainted the panel and placed in their minds that something "unlawful" happened the day of 27 April 2007. In fact, during the instruction about the order, the military judge used the word "unlawful" 11 times. This taint had a pour-over effect and caused the panel to therefore believe that SPC Sandoval's placing of command wire on the body of the deceased enemy combatant was also wrong and unlawful. Hence, because he followed an unlawful order, then at least something unlawful was going on the day of 27 April 2007. As such, anything else that was alleged by the government to have been unlawful must have been so as well. This improper panel instruction is legal error in the merits portion of the case that affects the validity of the findings.

In my clemency submission, I also referenced and enclosed an insightful opinion piece written in the *Wall Street Journal,* titled "Deadly Double Standards," as follows:

The enclosed article examines how some leaders in the

U.S. government and commanders have been judging "its young warriors for decisions they make in the heat of battle." After examining all of the evidence from the objective perspective of a panel member, the panel in the case of Sandoval came to much the same conclusion as the article that when it comes to applying the correct legal standard, those judging the actions of warriors in combat should recognize the tactical realities of an engagement. It may be legally and morally appropriate under certain circumstances to kill "unarmed" individuals, such as those actively acting as lookouts for the emplacement of improvised explosive devices (IEDs) or participating in the network of conspirators building such devices.

I also referenced and enclosed an insightful article which came out in the *Stars and Stripes* on 17 August 2007 examining the "Haditha Massacre" and Marine Lieutenant General James Mattis'[45] decision to not refer certain charges to court-martial. The article described Mattis' written decision as how to dispose of the case as follows:

Noting the difficulties in applying civilian standards to military circumstances, [Mattis] quoted the late Supreme Court Justice Oliver Wendell Holmes Jr., who served as an infantryman in the Civil War and described war as an "incommunicable experience." Holmes also said that "detached reflection cannot be demanded in the presence of an uplifted knife."

The full "incommunicable experience" quote from Judge Oliver Wendell Holmes: "We have shared the incommunicable experience of war. We felt, we still feel, the passion of life to its top. In our youths, our hearts were touched with fire."

---

45   This is the same James Mattis who was confirmed as the 26th United States Secretary of Defense on January 20, 2017.

I also pointed out "the realities of war and combat as we engage terrorism and terrorists in a fight for our nation's well-being and survival," and outlined the fact that "the realities are that on today's battlefield, the enemy does not show itself and hides among the civilian populace. This places our warfighters in difficult situations when asked to distinguish between friend or foe when they are being shot at."

In my clemency submission, I stated that Sandoval had taken responsibility for his actions and pointed out that the panel's decision to merely reduce his rank and retain him in the Army sent a powerful message that Sandoval was a good soldier. I also drew attention to the Good Soldier Book and letters submitted by his family and friends on his behalf.

Winston Churchill's wonderful quote seemed perfectly appropriate in this instance: "I would rather be right than consistent." And I noted that, "Those words ring true today just as they did in Churchill's time. Today is decision-making time and we are left with deciding the right thing to do today in the case of SPC Sandoval. Perhaps one of the greatest attributes of the military justice system is that at the end of the day, after the trial is done and the evidence evaluated in the light of day and upon examination by the defense, the same command who referred these charges to a general court-martial is the same command who now reviews what happened at that trial and is able make the decision as to how to now dispose of the charges. In this case, where to go and how to dispose of the charges is by moving forward, and forward is to make SPC Sandoval whole."

In closing, I wrapped up my clemency submission by pointing out the injustices that had occurred—the arrest and interrogation of Sandoval while he was home on leave; the illegal punishment administered to Sandoval while in confinement (the stripping of his rank and placing of him on work detail); and the egregiously premature labeling before trial of Sandoval as a "murderer" in the newspapers of his hometown of Laredo, Texas, his unit's home station's paper, and in the paper of his unit in theater, *The Stars and Stripes*. I noted that, "This was all done before he had the ability to put on a defense and be cleared of these allegations."

"As you make the determination on whether to grant clemency," I stated, "we ask that you consider all of these matters that we have presented here along with the record of trial and the letters from SPC Sandoval's family and friends. Clemency in this case would clearly communicate to SPC Sandoval and his family that he does have a future in society and that the mistake he made on the field of battle in Iraq, at the direction of his squad leader, does not have to haunt him in the form of a criminal record for the rest of his life. This request for clemency is not only in the best interests of SPC Sandoval, but in the interest of his family and the U.S. Army….Today, irrespective of consistency with prior action, is an opportunity to be right, and right is to disapprove this conviction and allow SPC Sandoval to move forward with his life and career. In light of the matters outlined above, the defense requests that you disapprove the court's finding of guilty, disapprove all punishments, and restore SPC Sandoval to the position he was in prior to referral of charges in this case."

Unfortunately, MG Lynch issued orders that fixed some minor administrative errors in the case and then issued an order that affirmed the entire conviction and granted no clemency relief to Sandoval. I do not know whether he personally read my clemency submission. Apparently, he thought the case and result was justice. One wonders if MG Lynch would have wanted to be judged by the same standard as was Sandoval. One wonders too whether he had ever shot someone on the field of battle or disciplined other soldiers for failing to follow his orders. The contradictions between the way Sandoval was judged, critiqued, and punished were in stark contrast to the actions of many of our senior military leadership, and the best way to describe it was that it was simply frustrating.

War is hell—and apparently, military justice can be as well.

EIGHTEEN - IN SANDOVAL'S WORDS

"Life is like riding a bicycle. To keep your balance you must keep moving."

~ Albert Einstein (Einstein: His Life and Universe, 2007)

"I always liked the idea of the military," recalls Sandoval in a 2016 interview for this book.

It intrigued me a lot. My father himself didn't serve in Vietnam but he had many friends who served in the military and they made an impression on me as I was growing up in the 1980s. I would see my dad's military friends wearing their old uniform jackets when it was cold and I'd ask questions about their time in the military. I began to realize that being in the military was a good thing.

As the years went by, I continued to like the idea of the military. When I was a high school freshman, I joined the JROTC program. That set it in stone for me—I was going to go into the military.

My mother was not a U.S. citizen. My father was a U.S. citizen and grew up in Texas, but his parents were born in Mexico. All his life he worked in the crop fields so he could save money and send it home to his parents. The United States gave my father the opportunity to work, and it also gave my mother the opportunity to support us kids after she and my dad separated and she became a single mother. Mom was really good to us, and we never wanted for anything. We may not have had much but we made do with what we had.

I appreciated everything this country had done for my family, and I wanted to do something in return. Serving in the military really appealed to me. I felt that it would be an honor to serve my country. I love the United States, and I had a calling to join the military. I knew I had to serve—and I really wanted to.

Near the end of the trial, I made a statement asking to be allowed to stay in the Army—and after the trial I did return to my unit in Alaska. Being back with my unit, I was concerned about the way some of them perceived me because of the trial. The people who had charged us with those crimes were still there. So, even though I was offered the opportunity to reenlist, I thought, *I don't want to be looked down upon or treated differently.* I knew that if I stayed, I would always be wondering who was looking at me weird.

We had a huge portion of the military and legal community supporting us, but a lot of people looked down on us. Their attitude was, "Well, that's what the headline said, so it must be true. You guys were charged with murder, so you must have been breaking laws and killing people." It was like some people thought that we killed for fun.

Some soldiers looked down on us and some turned away. I never knew what was going through people's heads. I would ask myself, *Did they decide on their own that I did something wrong? Or did they figure that since I was charged that meant I must be guilty?*

I even lost a few friends from the Army. I would be attending a hearing and run into a friend. When I tried to say hi, they would turn away. I wanted to say, "You know who I am. I trained next to you. We spent all those nights out in the cold, marching next to one another." I wondered if maybe someone in the chain of command was telling people, "This guy is on base and I don't want you to talk to him."

So I left the Army, took some time off from working, and lived off my savings. But my heart remained open to the military.

Shortly after I left the Army, I ran into one of my friends from high school who happened to be in the military. He was stationed in Germany but was home on leave.

"Hey! You out already?" he asked.

When I told him that I was no longer in the Army, he said, "Have you ever thought about joining the National Guard?"

"To be honest, no I haven't."

"Well, you should come by. We're getting ready to deploy sometime next year."

At first I didn't know what to think, but the more I thought about it, I realized I kind of missed the military. I only left because of what happened with the trial. I missed the camaraderie. I missed having a purpose in life.

So I joined the Texas Army National Guard in 2008, the same year I left the Army. I have been in the National Guard ever since. I have deployed to Iraq and Afghanistan and recently returned from a tour of duty in the Sinai Peninsula. Joining the National Guard filled a void and it was a way to cope with my life at the time. Before re-joining the military, I was starting to feel like, *Well, I guess that's it for me! I've reached my pinnacle!*

I had already done what I always wanted to do with my life. As I've said, from the time I was a child, I wanted to serve in the military. I wanted to be a soldier. That was who and what I wanted to be. After the trial, I felt that was taken away from me—even though I gave it up on my own.

I saw an opportunity to start new with the National Guard and I took it. When I found myself back in Iraq, I found myself more paranoid, more vigilant. I will always be more vigilant than before the trial. I am always aware now that I must take great care to make sure I'm in the right.

What happened will never completely be over for me. Those incidents will stay in my mind forever. We were in

Iraq serving in the military—something I wanted to do but many other people our age didn't want to do. We were put in real shitty situations and had to make decisions other kids our age didn't want to make. I was out there doing what I loved and having all those charges thrown at me felt like my service to the military was very underappreciated.

To be charged with murder made me feel like, *Wow! We are already here doing things normal kids our age wouldn't do, doing our military jobs, and this is what happens? This is how we're thanked? Our names are slapped across newspaper headlines and we're made out to be murderers?*

After Sandoval's trial, both Hensley and Vela were later tried, each separately. Hensley proceeded to trial and was acquitted of his murder charges, but found guilty of planting command wire on a body, and guilty of disrespect toward a superior officer. (The disrespect charge was unrelated to the events of 27 April or 11 May 2007 and related to disrespect toward one of the military officers of his unit.) He was sentenced to the time he had served in confinement (135 days), reprimanded, and demoted in rank.

Vela proceeded to trial and was ultimately found guilty of murder and other charges related to the 11 May 2007 incident. He was sentenced to ten years in prison at Fort Leavenworth and a dishonorable discharge from the Army.

Sandoval served his time in confinement, returned to his unit in Alaska, and later was honorably discharged from the Army and returned home to Laredo, Texas. After a brief period out of the military, Sandoval enlisted in the Texas Army National Guard, where he serves to this day.

On my end, I was awarded the Bronze Star for serving as a Trial Defense Counsel in Iraq and flying in and out of combat zones; continued to represent other combat soldiers charged with crimes; and months later returned back to Fort Bliss where I was assigned to the defense of my next clients.

No one else was ever court-martialed for crimes or wrongdoing for the actions on 27 April 2007 or 11 May 2007. The Commanding General, Rick Lynch, who ordered the courts-martial of Sandoval, Hensley, and Vela, and who denied Sandoval all clemency relief, was later promoted in rank to Lieutenant General and went on to hold higher commands. He has since retired from the service and written a book—apparently about his version of leadership. I will not be purchasing a copy.

On 15 December 2011, American troops officially ended the U.S. military mission in Iraq. As of 2016, U.S. troops are assigned to the numerous locations where they are designated by the Department of Defense to receive "imminent danger pay" for their service. This pay is given for formally undeclared wars and in combat operations with an oftentimes unclear enemy: Iraq, Afghanistan, Lebanon, Jordan, Pakistan, Syria, Yemen, and Egypt.

AFTERWORD

The battlefields of war upon which many of our grandparents and great-grandparents fought are no more. It is highly unlikely that there will ever again be clear lines on a battlefield with one side charging against the other on open plains or beaches. It is also unlikely that friend and foe alike will ever again be easily distinguishable on the field of battle. In today's armed conflicts, most units lack a common uniform and do not wave the flag of their unit or country overhead during their charge. Our military leaders—and, perhaps more importantly, the American public—must contend with and accept this new reality and the uncertainty of combat when we send our men and women to war.

We must not judge our men and women with 20/20 hindsight or after long, detached reflection for actions taken in seconds or minutes during battle. We must be willing to accept that war is truly hell and that the battlefields of the future are increasingly ambiguous and ones with no clear enemy.

For a military commander, it is easy to accuse a lowly Private of doing something wrong or to criticize the actions of a young soldier in the heat of battle. It is quite another thing to actually be the soldier in the heat of battle or to stand up and defend that soldier's actions. Senior military officers, who are oftentimes far removed from the actual battlefield, are quick to assign all the blame to the youngest soldiers because unfortunate combat events happened to make the news and they believe that someone must be held accountable.

When accused of a crime in a war-zone, oftentimes the only person able to defend that soldier is his military attorney. While some may choose to paint a wide-brush criticism of attorneys as the worst of society, I believe the law can be a highly noble profession if you are willing to fight hard for the right clients and the right causes. In all of our conflicts in Iraq, Afghanistan, Vietnam, and other locations, there have been, and continue to be, military lawyers and paralegals flying into dangerous places every day with one goal in mind—defending their client.

It was an honor to fight in a courtroom for Sandoval as he, and countless others, fought on the actual battlefields with our nation's flag proudly on their uniform. After all, this is the motto of the U.S. Army Trial Defense Service: "Defending those who defend America."

It was with these thoughts in mind that I believed the story of Sandoval and his actions while being assigned as a U.S. Army Sniper in The Triangle of Death—the most dangerous area of Iraq in 2007—needed to be told.

ABOUT THE AUTHOR

Craig W. Drummond is an attorney and former Captain in the U.S. Army JAG Corps. He is originally from the historic town of St. Joseph, Missouri, and received his undergraduate and law degrees from Drake University. In 2007 Captain Drummond was deployed to Iraq where he defended U.S. Army Sniper Specialist Jorge G. Sandoval, Jr. who was being court-martialed for two murders and other related charges. The case made international headlines with *The New York Times, The Washington Post, Los Angeles Times*, and the *Associated Press* all having reporters cover the trial. Captain Drummond was awarded the Bronze Star Medal for his service in Iraq. While on active duty, Captain Drummond served in various assignments, to include as a Military Prosecutor (Trial Counsel), Trial Defense Counsel (TDS), and Brigade Judge Advocate (BJA). In 2010 Captain Drummond was honorably discharged from the Army.

The author currently resides in Las Vegas, Nevada, where he practices law, defending citizens charged with crimes and those injured by the negligence of others. He is actively involved with the Nevada Veterans community and when not in trial, he spends every spare second with his amazing wife and two sons.

More information about the author can be found at DrummondFirm.com.

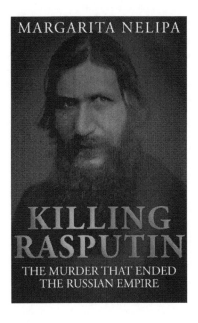

 **WILDBLUE PRESS**

See even more at:
http://wbp.bz/tc

More True Crime You'll Love From WildBlue Press

BOGEYMAN: He Was Every Parent's Nightmare by Steve Jackson *"A master class in true crime reporting. He writes with both muscle and heart."* (Gregg Olsen, New York Time bestselling author). A national true crime bestseller about the efforts of tenacious Texas lawmen to solve the cold case murders of three little girls and hold their killer accountable for his horrific crimes by New York Times bestselling author Steve Jackson. *"Absorbing and haunting!"* (Ron Franscell, national bestselling author and journalist)

wbp.bz/bogeyman

REPEAT OFFENDER by Bradley Nickell *"Best True Crime Book of 2015"* (Suspense Magazine) A "Sin City" cop recounts his efforts to catch one of the most prolific criminals to ever walk the neon-lit streets of Las Vegas. *"If you like mayhem, madness, and suspense, Repeat Offender is the book to read."* (Aphrodite Jones, New York Times bestselling author)

wbp.bz/ro

DADDY'S LITTLE SECRET by Denise Wallace *"An engrossing true story."* (John Ferak, bestselling author of Failure Of Justice, Body Of Proof, and Dixie's Last Stand) Daddy's Little Secret is the poignant true crime story about a daughter who, upon her father's murder, learns of his secret double-life. She had looked the other way about other hidden facets of his life - deadly secrets that could help his killer escape the death penalty, should she come forward.

wbp.bz/dls

BODY OF PROOF by John Ferak *"A superbly crafted tale of murder and mystery."* – (Jim Hollock, author of award-winning BORN TO LOSE) When Jessica O'Grady, a tall, starry-eyed Omaha co-ed, disappeared in May 2006, leaving behind only a blood-stained mattress, her "Mr. Right," Christopher Edwards, became the suspect. Forensic evidence gathered by CSI stalwart Dave Kofoed, a man driven to solve high-profile murders, was used to convict Edwards. But was the evidence tainted? A true crime thriller written by bestselling author and award-winning journalist John Ferak.

wbp.bz/bop

Made in the USA
Columbia, SC
01 April 2018